50 Ways to Love Your Friends

Approaching the Heart with a Rational Mind

Sarah Cline, Ph.D.

Copyright © 2023 Sarah Cline, Ph.D. All rights reserved.

The contents of this book may not be reproduced, duplicated, or transmitted without direct written permission from the author.

Under no circumstances will any legal responsibility or blame be held against the publisher for any reparation, damages, or monetary loss due to the information herein, either directly or indirectly.

Legal Notice:

This book is copyright-protected. This is only for personal use. You cannot amend, distribute, sell, use, quote, or paraphrase any part of the content within this book without the consent of the author.

Disclaimer Notice:

Please note the information contained within this document is for educational and entertainment purposes only. Every attempt has been made to provide accurate, up-to-date, and reliable complete information. No warranties of any kind are expressed or implied. Readers acknowledge that the author is not engaging in the rendering of legal, financial, medical, or professional advice. The content of this book has been derived from various sources. Please consult a licensed professional before attempting any techniques outlined in this book.

By reading this document, the reader agrees that under no circumstances is the author responsible for any losses, direct or indirect, which are incurred as a result of the use of the information contained within this document, including, but not limited to, errors, omissions, or inaccuracies.

ISBN: 978-1-937209-22-3

Contents

Introduction	1
1. Understanding Personality Types: A Deep Dive	3
Origins of Personality Types	
Cave Dweller (CD) and Mountain Yeller (MY)	
So, How Do You Find Common Ground?	
Key Takeaways	
2. Communication Is Everything	17
Express Feelings Without Instigating Conflicts	
Prioritize Active Listening	
Use Neutral Language to Curb Defensiveness	
Understand That Friendship Dynamics Change	
Understand and Respect New Boundaries as Transitions Occur	
Check in With Them Often	
Catch Up and Share Your Own Journey	
Respect Their Space and Yours	
Apologize When Necessary	
Create Open and Honest Dialogue	
Key Takeaways:	
3. Strengthen Your Bonds	38
Give Compliments	

    Offer Surprise Gestures
    Walk Down Memory Lane
    Use Your Skills
    Hug Them
    Write Them Letters
    Make New Memories
    Delve into Mutual Hobbies
    Bring Them Thoughtful Gifts
    Make Your Own Traditions
    Express Your Appreciation
    Be Vulnerable
    Key Takeaways:

4. Celebrate Your Friend   53
    Invite Them Over for a Friend Night or a Party
    Remember Important Dates
    Honor Them
    Share Music with Each Other
    Encourage Self-Care
    Practice Inclusion
    Explore Each Other's Neighborhoods
    Share in Their Joys
    Respect Their Time
    Surprise Them
    Key Takeaways:

5. Appreciate Them for Who They Are   66
    Celebrate Their Emotional Strengths
    Understand That They're Human—Just Like You
    Learn About Their Story
    Encourage Their Future Aspirations

      Celebrate Their Uniqueness
      Key Takeaways:

6. Friendship Fences   75
      Set Appropriate Boundaries as Your Friendship Evolves
      Ask for Advice and Listen When They Give It
      Respect Differences
      Don't Forget "You Time"
      Be Consistent
      Key Takeaways:

7. Social Time   85
      Exercise Together
      Let Them Confide in You
      Have Inside Jokes
      Try New Restaurants Together
      Be Reliable
      Be Flexible
      Revisit Places of Significance
      Key Takeaways:

8. Chapter 8: Final Thoughts   104
      Above Everything Else, Communicate
      We Are All Human
      Respect Differences
      Take Responsibility
      Stop Making Assumptions
      Stay in Contact and Practice Being Present, Even When There's Conflict

9. Appendices   109

Self-Assessment Questionnaire: Determine if You're a CD, MY, or Straddler.
Personality Indicator #1
Personality Indicator #2
Personality Indicator Scores
Using the Scoring Chart
Cave Dweller Tendencies
Cave Dweller Priorities
Mountain Yeller Tendencies
Mountain Yeller Priorities

Introduction

Friendships can be complicated sometimes, but they don't have to be. By picking up this guide you are taking a brave first step toward understanding and enhancing your relationship with your friends. Within these pages, we will delve into three distinct personality types that shape relationships. They include the reserved Cave Dweller, the outgoing Mountain Yeller, and the Straddler, who exhibits traits from both personality types. With practical insights and real-life examples of these personalities, you will have a whole arsenal at your disposal to help you navigate the dynamics of any relationship while also gaining a deeper understanding of yourself. So, get ready to see your friends—and perhaps even yourself—in a whole new light as we explore 50 Ways to Love Your Friends.

Buckle up for the ride, because we're about to uncover the mysteries of CDs (Cave Dwellers), MYs (Mountain Yellers), and Straddlers. Think of it as a personality safari, where we'll observe these fascinating creatures in their natural habitat and gain a deeper understanding of each type as well as explore how they might pertain to everyday situations. Armed with this knowledge, you'll be able to decode your friends' behaviors skillfully and avoid misunderstandings. No more of the blame game when it comes to miscommunication—it's all about recognizing and respecting our inherent differences with a little empathy and patience. So, let's hop on this wild ride and learn how to better connect with our friends!

Forget the quick fixes and checklists because loving others is an active effort. This book will guide you, but it's up to you to truly apply these insights. It may require some soul-searching and challenge your current beliefs, but the payoff is worth it—because that payoff is a deeper bond and a better understanding of yourself and those you love.

Chapter One

Understanding Personality Types: A Deep Dive

Do you find yourself needing help understanding the personality traits of your loved ones? Do you ever feel frustrated that they seem dissimilar to you? Or, what about being frustrated that they're so similar to yourself? What about your friend? Do you feel the need to understand them more?

Understanding personality types is an essential piece of the puzzle when seeking to understand others—and your best friends are no exception to that. Appreciating them means discovering their true layers and complexities, and all of them should garner your attention if you are ever to experience a happy and healthy relationship.

In this chapter, we will discuss the personality types of the Cave Dweller, the Mountain Yeller, and the Straddler. Learning about these three basic personality types will give you a clearer picture of the unique benefits and challenges each creates. Understanding these personality types is an essential first step to bringing harmony and happiness into your everyday life.

Origins of Personality Types

Before the modern-day classifications of CDs and MYs and even before psychiatrists and psychologists stepped onto the scene, ancient civilizations sought to explain human behavior and its various nuances.

The Ancient Greeks

The ancient Greeks developed the theory of "four humors" to explain the causes of health and illness, both mental and physical. This theory suggested that an individual's temperament was influenced by bodily fluids: blood (sanguine), yellow bile (choleric), black bile (melancholic), and phlegm (phlegmatic). The Greeks thought these humors were directly related to being sanguine (cheerful), choleric (short-tempered), melancholic (reserved), or phlegmatic (relaxed). Therefore, the balance of these humors was believed to influence an individual's temperament, health, and overall disposition. An imbalance of these humors led to behaviors that, today, we associate with certain mental illnesses. For example:

- Sanguine (blood) was associated with cheerful, optimistic, enthusiastic personality traits. An imbalance was thought to be due to a person having too much blood in their body, which would cause them to be overly confident and have impulsive behavior. Possible narcissistic and bipolar disorder.

- Choleric (yellow bile) was associated with being ambitious, passionate, and easily angered. An imbalance causes anger, irritability, or extremely aggressive behavior and rage. Possible borderline personality disorder.

- Melancholic (black bile) was associated with being thoughtful, reflective, and often sad or depressed. This imbalance was associated with melancholy and depression.

- Phlegmatic (phlegm) was associated with being calm, reliable, and often unemotional or apathetic. An imbalance was associated with lethargy, sluggishness, or a lack of motivation, which, much like melancholia, is a symptom of depression.

Treating these emotional ailments is where things got even more interesting. If the Greeks thought you had an imbalance of any of these four humors, you would likely have received one of the following treatments:

Dietary Changes: Prescribed depending on the humor in excess. For instance, someone deemed overly choleric might be advised to avoid hot or spicy foods that would "agitate" the yellow bile.

Bloodletting: If you were someone believed to have an excess of sanguine humor, it was common practice to be prescribed bloodletting. This process involved removing blood from the body by way of leeches or actual cutting.

Purging: To remove excess bile or phlegm, laxatives were used, as were emetics, which induced vomiting.

Baths/Sweating: To promote toxin removal, balms and ointments were applied to the skin to help imbalance these four humors.

The Greeks' attempts to "treat" imbalances in personality or health were based on the observations and the knowledge they had at the time. The four humors theory was eventually replaced with more accurate medical models, but its influence can still be seen in some of our languages today.

The Introvert and the Extrovert

Carl Gustav Jung (1875–1961) was a Swiss psychiatrist, psychoanalyst, and the father of analytical psychology. He developed several concepts that had a profound influence on both psychology and popular culture. One of his most notable contributions was the concept of "introversion" and "extraversion" (often used in the more modern manner: introvert and extrovert). Jung's theory asserts that introversion and extraversion are attitudes that represent the direction in which a person's psychic energy flows.

Extraversion (Extrovert)

According to Jung, the extrovert's energy flows outward. This personality type is more oriented toward the external world and derives energy from interacting with its surroundings, including people, events, and situations. If your friend is an extrovert, they tend to be more outgoing, social, and interested in external events. They are typically action-oriented and more comfortable in social situations than an introverted friend. External factors influence extroverts, who are occasionally prone to negative introspection.

Introversion (Introvert)

As the name suggests, the introvert's energy flows inward. This personality type is more oriented toward her inner world, relying on introspection and internal reflection. If your friend is introverted, they are generally more reserved and often feel more comfortable with individual activities or smaller group settings. They derive energy and pleasure from thinking, daydreaming, or exploring ideas. Although an introverted person's daily practices tend to lead to social isolation, they tend to have a small number of deep connections with people of their choosing.

Jung believed that everyone has an introverted and extroverted side, with one being more dominant than the other. It's a spectrum, and while some people might be near the extremes of that spectrum, most individuals lie somewhere in between.

Cave Dweller (CD) and Mountain Yeller (MY)

While not strictly rooted in these historical contexts, the CD and MY classifications are evolved constructs reflecting the same human desire to understand ourselves and others in our world more deeply.

While our contemporary understanding of the CD and MY classifications doesn't stem directly from ancient Greek or Jungian theories, much like their historical counterparts, they are observed patterns in modern relationships. By identifying recurring patterns, we can forge tools to help us navigate and harmonize interpersonal interactions.

Cave Dweller (CD)

We must first learn about their traits to determine where you and your friend fall; CD or MY.

Reserved Nature

If your friend is a CD, they will predominantly be calm and reserved. CDs are introspective and tend to hold their emotions close to their chest because they value their inner world and the sanctuary it provides. Their reserved nature doesn't mean that they are indifferent or don't care about those around them; it just means that they process their emotions internally and over time.

For instance, after an argument, a CD might withdraw to process their feelings rather than immediately confront an issue. A CD does this because they typically feel uncomfortable with strife and need time to work through their emotions and understand how to communicate their feelings.

Socially, a CD is often found in quieter corners, engaging in deep conversation with one or two individuals rather than in the center of a party. In group discussions, a CD will offer insights only if specifically asked or if they feel strongly about a topic.

Logical Thinking and Literal Communication

A CD leans more toward analytical and logical thinking. They make decisions only after careful contemplation and weighing the pros and cons. They work hard to keep their emotions from clouding their judgment. This logical thinking manifests in their communication; they will get to the point without inserting emotions or using stories to embellish their point.

For example, if you discuss a film with a CD, they will likely dissect plot points with impeccable logic and even point out strengths and weaknesses, but they often miss the emotional undertones of the movie. If you ask a CD if they liked the cake you brought for dessert, they might reply, "Yes," without diving into flowery descriptives.

It's important to note that a CD may also get frustrated with an embellished story that takes longer to get to the point. It doesn't mean they don't want to hear the story or don't care what you have to say; their brain is just geared toward immediate outcomes.

Need for Space

A CD has an inherent need for emotional and physical personal space. For them, requiring space is not about distancing themselves from loved ones. It's about needing solitude to recharge and reflect.

CDs enjoy reading books in a cozy nook or going for solitary walks. They may listen to music while cooking dinner instead of talking. This alone time is essential for a CD, especially after a day filled with social interactions.

Singular Focus

A CD has unparalleled concentration when engrossed in a task and prefers completing that task to their satisfaction before tackling another.

If you attempt to talk to a CD while they're writing an email, for example, they may be so absorbed in what they're writing that you'll be tuned out. It's not that what you're saying is unimportant to them; it's just challenging for them to spread their focus on more than one thing at a time because they give each item their full attention.

Social Preferences

Traditionally, if your friend is labeled an introvert, others would consider them anti-social. But that couldn't be farther from the truth. An introvert, or a CD, just leans toward more intimate social interactions. Large gatherings can overwhelm a CD and drain their mental and emotional battery.

Emotional Processing

While CDs might not outwardly express their emotions, they experience them *deeply*. However, their internal reflections may lead to a delay in their outward emotional expression. While a CD may seem distant after an emotional confrontation, they must process the interaction before reacting. A CD needs time to contemplate a disagreement, analyze the conversation, and figure out where things went wrong before they can move on to a resolution. This meditation is essential for a CD's loved one to understand; the more you push them to express themselves, the more they will clam up in response.

Mountain Yeller (MY)

If your friend is an extrovert, chances are they've been called that more than once in their lifetime. An extrovert is typically known for being outgoing and the life of any party. But there's so much more to them than meets the eye.

Outgoing Nature/Group Socialization

An MY is inherently outgoing. Their energy thrives on interactions and being around people as often as possible. Instead of needing time alone to recharge, MYs wants to be out and involved.

At a social event, MYs will be the first to initiate games and dancing and will often bounce from person to person, catching up rather than focusing on one task at a time. Deep conversations are still on the table, but not at a social event. An MY usually rallies their friends for a group outing over a weekend rather than sitting at home reading a book or watching TV. Even in the workplace, MYs love group projects and find collaborative brainstorming and teamwork exciting.

Emotion-Driven

MYs are heart-ruled because they lead with their intuition and emotions. Being ruled by their heart doesn't mean their decisions are devoid of logic, but their feelings heavily influence their reactions. An MY can be emotional during arguments but is also the first to send a heartfelt message to a friend or family member upon hearing they are having a rough time.

An MYs emotions will show throughout their storytelling, so be patient when they tell you about an event or relay the plot to a movie. Chances are both will be full of details and embellishments.

Connection and Touch

MYs crave genuine connections and physical touch. Whether it be a hug, a pat on the back, or simply holding hands, physical touch reinforces their feeling of being connected. In relating with you, an MY will crave physical affection and see it as a top priority over other needs—something we'll discuss in depth a bit later.

Dynamic Focus

An MY is a natural multitasker. Instead of focusing on one task at a time, their attention shifts between assignments. They enjoy the energy they get from juggling multiple things and often get bored working on one project for an extended period.

An MY doesn't mind dealing with paperwork but works through it while watching television or listening to music. As for conversations, an MY loves to chat, but don't be surprised if you find them scrolling on their phone while talking with you. It's not that they think what you have to say is unimportant; their mind simply just runs at a faster rate than a CD, making them more comfortable processing more than one thing at a time.

Inferential Communication

An MY often communicates using stories, anecdotes, and metaphors rather than getting straight to the point. They rely on indirect implications and expect others to infer meanings, which can confuse some who aren't familiar with their communication style.

During an argument, someone may find it hard to decipher what the MY really wants, even if they feel they have told them directly. It's essential to have a middle ground where communication is concerned, especially if your friend is an MY and you are a CD. Because the communication styles between personalities are very different.

Immediate Emotional Expression

Unlike their CD counterparts, MYs are quick to express their emotions. They're an open book and rarely hesitate to share their feelings of joy and disappointment. This can be overwhelming for a CD uncomfortable with an emotional display.

One of the greatest fears an MY faces is the fear of rejection. If an MY has a CD child who usually pulls away at any sign of conflict, this can be a bone of contention. An MY will take a withdrawal from the friendship as a sign of personal rejection. It's important to communicate that you are not rejecting them and need time to wrap your head around and process things. Give the MY verbal and physical affirmations whenever possible.

If you are a CD and your friend is an MY, don't panic; it doesn't mean you cannot have a successful relationship. There are plenty of amazing and fulfilling relationships between opposites. It just means it will take time, work, and patience to learn one another's needs and effectively communicate.

The Straddler

If your friend is a Straddler, they are adaptable and enjoy the best of both worlds. They can immerse themselves in a book like a CD or be the life of a party like an MY. They possess an emotional agility that allows them to straddle their personality types seamlessly. While this book predominantly focuses on CD and MY, Straddlers can use it to understand the extremes and navigate their middle ground more effectively.

Excellent Balance between Reflection and Expression

A Straddler can introspect like a CD, valuing quiet moments of thought. Yet, they also appreciate the expressive vitality that an MY has and share their feelings and ideas openly when a situation calls for it. They are as happy spending a quiet evening reading and attending a book club as they are actively participating in a lively discussion.

Adaptable in Social Situations

While they might not always be the life of the party, they easily adjust to situations based on the social settings and the company involved. They can engage in a one-on-one conversation at a party and then join a group game or be at the party's center later in the evening.

Values: Both Logic and Emotion

A Straddler approaches situations with a logical mindset but is equally attuned to the emotional undercurrents, valuing the importance of feelings in decision-making. For example, if a friend faces a personal issue, the Straddler will offer practical solutions while providing emotional support.

Flexibility in Needs and Fears

The Straddler's hierarchy of needs will fluctuate based on circumstances, and they might experience the same fears from a CD's spectrum, such as loss of security, as well as the MY's fear of rejection. However, adaptability allows them to prioritize different aspects of their life. While working on an important business project, they will prioritize career stability, but in downtime, they will focus on relationships and personal connections.

Fluid Communication Styles

A Straddler can communicate directly and inferentially, often adjusting communication based on the recipient. For example, when conversing with an analytical boss, they will be direct and to the point, but when they talk to their best friend, they become expressive and delve into all the nitty-gritty details.

Straddlers possess an innate ability to mediate and find common ground, especially in relationships where CDs and MYs might find themselves at odds. Their adaptability enables them to comprehend and empathize with both personality types, easing communication and diminishing misunderstandings.

A Straddler may seem like the perfect personality type. However, everyone encounters their share of struggles. The flexibility of a Straddler often confuses their preferences and needs. The Straddler might sometimes feel stretched or trapped in the middle, particularly in a polarized situation where they wish to please others so much that they struggle to voice their disagreements. A Straddler must discern what is truly significant to them while learning to navigate other personality types, much like everyone else.

So, How Do You Find Common Ground?

"I'm a CD, and my friend is an MY; is my relationship with them doomed?" No! In this book, we don't tell you how to "cope" with differences. We allow you to realize each person's unique strengths in a relationship. A CD's introspection can balance an MY's spontaneity. An MY's vivacity and exuberance can harmonize beautifully with a CD's depth and stability.

Recognizing these different traits is merely the first step to a healthy relationship. The real challenge, and indeed the focus of this book, is to find ways to navigate the complexities of these interactions. After all, the beauty of a relationship truly unfolds in the dance between these personalities.

Key Takeaways

Diving into the intricacies of personality types isn't about affixing labels but enriching our understanding. With these insights, you're now armed with the necessary vocabulary to navigate the labyrinth of human emotions and connections, fostering an environment where love thrives, understanding blossoms, and relationships flourish. As we traverse this journey, let's remember that the goal isn't to change but to adapt, understand, and love more deeply.

The foundation for a nurturing relationship starts with understanding—understanding yourself, your friend, and the dynamics of your interaction with one another. With the knowledge of CD and MY personality traits, you're well on your way to deepening that understanding, setting the stage for the subsequent chapters that will guide you on how to cherish your friend in ways that resonate with both of you.

Understanding personality differences is essential for nurturing compatibility. This chapter has illuminated the fundamental traits of CDs, MYs, and Straddlers.

- **Reserved Nature:** Respect your CD friend's need for personal space and quiet reflection. Don't force immediate emotional reactions.

- **Logical Thinking:** Recognize your CD friend's analytical approach. Be patient as they process before expressing feelings.

- **Singular Focus:** Acknowledge that multitasking is difficult for your CD friend. Allow them to complete or pause their task before they give you their full attention.

- **Emotion-Driven:** Empathize with your MY friend's emotions. Give them positive affirmations/compliments and physical affection.

- **Inferential Communication:** Listen for meanings implied indirectly in your MY friend's stories. Learn to read between the lines.

- **Dynamic Focus:** Accept your MY friend's wandering attention. Multitasking is in their nature. However, if you need their full focus, tell them.

- **Excellent Balance:** Appreciate the adaptability of a Straddler but avoid putting them in the middle of conflicts.

- **Flexible Needs:** Accommodate shifts in a Straddler's priorities. Reassure them of your unconditional love.

Chapter Two

Communication Is Everything

Effective communication is the foundation of any healthy relationship, regardless of if it is a romantic relationship or a relationship with your friend. It also does not discriminate against personality type. Communication is the bridge that connects us all—whether we are CDs or MYs. It enables us to come to a mutual understanding and build a stronger bond.

In this chapter, we'll delve into the essential components of communication that can strengthen the bond you have with your friend. Moreover, the chapter will navigate the traits of each personality type and how you can use personality indicators to validate your friend, yourself, and both of your needs.

While it's easy to be swayed by the idea that love is a mysterious force beyond our control, the reality is that maintaining a lasting relationship requires a lot more than just love. It requires conscious effort, respect, and a willingness to understand one another on a deeper level. This journey of appreciation goes beyond knowing your friend's favorite things or doing what you think will make them happy. It's about diving deep into their psyche (and yours), comprehending their unique personality traits (and yours), and recognizing how their attributes interact with yours in a way that can formulate a healthy and lasting relationship.

In the age of digital connections and instant gratification, we sometimes forget the beauty of human interaction. We often overlook the importance of patience, reflection, and presence with our loved ones. At times, we also let external factors beyond that pull us away from what truly matters. Thus, you can pause, reflect, and feel as we progress through this chapter. By fostering an environment of open communication and mutual respect, you're not just building relationships and bonds but cultivating relationships that thrive on understanding, compassion, and genuine connection. Using this guide, you can learn how to communicate with your friend and establish some strategies to help you convey your emotions effectively:

Express Feelings Without Instigating Conflicts

Expressing your feelings is crucial for any relationship, but it's also essential to do so without triggering conflicts. It's too easy to get wrapped up in emotions when expressing them to someone else—especially when you're first sorting through them—so it's crucial to take a step back, breathe, and formulate thoughts before verbalizing them. Sometimes tensions are high, and although we all like to think we won't have conflicts with our friends, usually one or two will arise during our friendship. As an adult, you may think that you're able to lay everything out on the table and be completely honest. While this can be true—and even beneficial for your mental well-being—it is important to understand how to do it healthily. Make sure to keep the heightened emotions to a minimum to avoid conflict as much as possible.

Remain Calm

Try not to overreact to difficult situations. By remaining calm, it's more likely that your friend will respect you enough to see your perspective.

Express Feelings with Words, Not Actions

If you start to get angry and feel you may lose control, take a break, and do something to help yourself feel calm. For example, you could take a walk, do breathing exercises, interact with a pet, journal, or read a book.

Address One Issue at a Time

Only introduce tertiary issues once the primary problem has been fully discussed. This way, you'll avoid what experts call the "kitchen sink effect." Dr. John Mordechai Gottman (born April 26, 1942), an American psychologist and professor at the University of Washington, coined the term to describe the act of one person in a discussion or argument throwing "everything but the kitchen sink" into it by dredging up past mistakes and grievances. This tactic is particularly counterproductive as it's often overwhelming to the person receiving the grievances. This is also true of friendships. Even if you have a ton of grievances with your best friend, avoid bringing them all up during a time of argument or debate. These conversations are better suited to planned discussions.

Resist Underhandedness

Avoid hitting below the belt or being underhanded. Tensions can run high in any sort of relationship, and it may seem easy to hit below the belt when upset. But don't use these conversations to attack your friend. There are likely sensitive areas that could easily trigger them, or even hurt their feelings—and although this may be tempting in the moment, avoid it. These attacks only foster distrust, anger, and harmful vulnerability. We don't want to "win" arguments. We want to work through issues by effectively communicating.

Avoid Clamming Up

Positive results can only be obtained by way of proper communication. It's easy to feel emotionally charged when discussing your feelings with others and as these emotions run high, it's easy to shut down or "clam up."

It's important to note that when one person becomes silent and stops responding, frustration and anger can quickly follow. If you feel overwhelmed or as though you're shutting down, you may need to take a break from the discussion. Just remember to follow up where you left off later. Likewise, respect the fact that it may be your friend who needs the space.

Be Specific and Productive

Be specific about what is bothering you. Try not to generalize. Avoid words such as "never" or "always." These sweeping terms are usually inaccurate and will (almost) always heighten tensions. Instead of using hyperbolic language, focus on what you're feeling in the moment. Vague complaints are also challenging to address, and tackling each specific item productively is important.

Prioritize Active Listening

Practice active listening when others communicate with you. Avoid interrupting them when they're speaking, even if you disagree. Active listening is the cornerstone of all effective communication—and relationships in general. Active listening involves not only hearing the words people say but also understanding their emotions and perspectives. Validate them and show them that you're listening by maintaining eye contact and providing non-verbal cues like nodding. Our body language matters.

Be present in the conversation and take your friend's feelings and criticisms seriously. Don't be distracted by external forces. Never multitask while someone is communicating with you, and listen to and reflect on what they are saying before responding. Be sure to ask open-ended questions to encourage them to share more, and remember one thing: if they are communicating it, it's important.

Use Neutral Language to Curb Defensiveness

Your choice of words can significantly impact the tone of your communication. To prevent defensiveness and promote understanding, avoid accusatory language, and instead focus on the specific behavior or issue. Accusations will lead your friends to focus more on defending themselves rather than understanding you or your perspective. That is not a desired goal. Instead, discuss how an action or event made you *feel*.

Use "We" Statements

Using "we" instead of "you" statements conveys that you are in this together, working as a team to resolve a problem. Relationships are a two-way street, so what better way to show that you're trying to expand your relationship? It is important to communicate that you are practicing empathy as well as acknowledging their feelings and perspectives.

Don't Say This:

"You never understand where I'm coming from." This is a generalization. Your friend may know where you're coming from at times and saying otherwise is a good way to halt the conversation from desired outcomes. This puts an immediate negative connotation on the conversation and also puts them into defensive mode.

Instead, Say This:

"We seem to have a disconnect sometimes in our communication." Emphasizing "we" makes the conversation more about finding solutions together rather than pointing fingers, which can often lead to a more productive and less confrontational discussion.

Use "I" Statements

Expressing yourself without becoming overly aggressive can be challenging when faced with a conflict, especially if your friend is pushing your buttons. To help de-escalate the situation and clarify your point, an "I" or an assertive statement is an effective psychiatrist-approved approach. Suppose there's a conflict where you feel your friends are always getting involved with your life in ways you don't necessarily want them to be involved:

Don't Say This:

"You are always trying to tell me what to do." Again, this is a generalization and carries a negative connotation.

Instead, Say This:

"I feel a little overwhelmed when you assert your opinion or offer unsolicited advice. I would like us to set boundaries for this so we can always be on the same page."

This "I" statement expresses your feelings and needs without blaming or accusing them. After all, if you're having this conversation, it's because your friend wants to help—even when you don't want them to. Using language that emphasizes how you feel is much more effective communication and is less likely to result in them shutting down or getting angry. It also aids in their ability to empathize and see things from your perspective. Here's another example:

Don't Say This:

"You never listen to me." This is also a generalization.

Instead, Say This:

"I feel frustrated when I feel unheard. I would like it if we worked on listening to each other a little more effectively." This type of communication makes it so that each of you has something to work on. After all, we all could use a little extra help in effective communication and active listening.

Speaking this way also avoids tactics of attack, critique, and criticism, which usually lead to more hostility and defensiveness. In general, using "I" messages can create a constructive dialogue about the true causes of any conflict by avoiding aggressive behaviors and fostering effective communication.

Understand That Friendship Dynamics Change

We have all been there. One minute you're seeing your best friend all the time and the next you're lucky to go out to lunch once a month. Friends drift apart for various reasons, but with this guide, hopefully, you can put a ceasefire on the drift. At the end of the day, we're all busy. It's possible that you just don't have the time for each other like you used to. But even if that is the case, you can make the time you do have together a great experience that is fulfilling to your emotional needs. While it's normal for relationships to change over time, it can still be hard to adjust to.

Give It Some Time

If your friend is a co-worker or a classmate, leaving these environments can cause a little bit of a clash in your routine. Maybe you even moved areas, or maybe you've gotten married and/or had kids, and you just realize that the dynamic is changing.

Initially, after transitions such as this, there are clashes in routine. These differences can make it difficult to see each other as regularly as you're used to. It's possible to feel confused, sad, or even angry when you start to see less of a person who has been a big support to you before.

Give yourself time and space to work through any emotions that come up. If this is a friendship you want to maintain, have a conversation and work out a plan when you're levelheaded. This will prevent any sort of charged conversations that hold negativity. It is also important to allow time and space for your friend to adjust to the changed relationship.

Talk About How You're Feeling

This guide discusses the importance of vulnerability a little later, but for now, it's important to mention that you need to let your friend know how you're feeling during dynamic change or transition. Whenever you go through some big feelings, it's a good idea to talk with someone. Keeping it all locked inside can make you feel like you're carrying around the weight of the world.

While it's not easy, you should consider sharing how you've been feeling with the friend you're not seeing so much of anymore. Let them know how you feel about it and any suggestions you might have (if you have any). You might find they feel the same way and you can both work out a way to stay a part of each other's lives and shift with the times. This type of communication really helps us not only get to the bottom of our emotions but also how to work through difficult times together.

Understand and Respect New Boundaries as Transitions Occur

After you discuss changes with your friend, understand that transitions constantly happen, because changes are constantly occurring. Keep in mind that with that, boundaries are likely to change, too, right along with the relationship. Even if you haven't had a discussion about it yet, there are likely new boundaries in place that are different from the ones that existed when you first started your friendship.

Maybe one or both of you are married, and maybe that includes kids. Or, maybe the two of you are just growing and maturing as time goes on. Whatever the case, there is a high chance that the same boundaries that applied when you became first friends are different than the boundaries each of you have placed on yourselves and your friendship now.

At their best, friendships can be wonderful and accepting relationships that keep us emotionally fulfilled and in a mentally safe space. However, at their worst, they can be just as harsh and toxic as any other abusive relationship. It's important to spot the differences and make sure each of you has placed healthy boundaries on the other person. Make sure that you're communicating what new boundaries need to be in place as changes occur. Some examples of common boundaries to discuss consist of:

- **Significant Others:** It's possible that when you two became friends, you gave your opinion on anything and everything, including boyfriends/girlfriends/dates/etc. However, if this friend is in a serious relationship or vice versa, it's possible you/they don't want an opinion on your/their relationship or the things that pertain to it. After all, friends typically vent to one another, and it's possible you wouldn't see their significant other in the same light as they do when they aren't upset. Your friend may be hurt by a negative opinion of their significant other. Discuss what is fair game and what isn't—but remember, there's a fine line here, too. If you truly suspect your friend is in danger—whether mentally or physically—make sure you give them your opinion anyway and seek support and aid.

- **Raising Kids:** No two people are going to raise kids the same. Rearing children is not a one-size-fits-all dynamic. It's tough work and oftentimes takes a lot of learning on the fly. It also takes a lot of patience and understanding between two people who parented the child. No one needs a third wheel when raising a child. This can lead to major flare-ups if people start to disagree. If you or your friend has a child, make sure you discuss what is on or off limits when discussing your children (if it isn't obvious).

- **Financials:** Not many people want or need financial advice. Remember that unless your friend asks you for help, you probably shouldn't give your opinion.

- **When You Can Come Over**: If your friend has a family, make sure you're respecting their boundary and space. Make sure it's OK before you just stop in. You never know what someone has going on and you can't make assumptions that you are welcome, even if you used to be welcome at all times before the family came into the picture.

Check in With Them Often

There are huge benefits to checking in with others. It's important to perform emotional check-ins with your friend, where the two of you sit down during a consistent and regular time to ask how one another is doing and to get feedback on how the friendship is going. This is particularly beneficial in relationships where you might feel your communication is lacking at times, or you don't see each other as often as you would like. Whether it's scheduled or not, make sure that you are checking in on your friend.

Checking in at the right time can help your friend overcome challenges. This is because it helps them feel more valued, loved, and cherished. It also is a great opportunity for them to discuss anything bothering them. It's also great for you and your friendship because:

- Check-ins allow you to connect with others and can strengthen your bond.

- Checking in can help you to open up and become more self-aware about yourself and your own life.

- Having insight into each other's successes—as well as failures—can be a powerful opportunity to learn and grow, whether that be individually or together.

Self-reflection can be really powerful and also set the foundation that will allow you to check in with others as well. Self-reflection is an opportunity to look in the mirror and ask questions and learn how to empathize with others. Self-reflection is the act of thinking about your own thoughts, actions, motivations, beliefs, and your impact on others. Benefits of it include:

- Readying yourself to share your own struggles as well as your successes.

- Identifying whether you're in a healthy position to support others.

- Identifying what you need to do to progress in the future by identifying areas of weakness.

How to Check in With Friends

If you have found that you're unable to properly check in with your friends because your own mental health isn't good, then start simple.

Send a text or make a phone call. They don't have to be grand or time-consuming. However, if you would like something a little more intimate, ask them out for coffee or lunch. Whichever sort of format you choose, make sure you:

- **Are Prepared to Be Vulnerable**: Sharing with your friend is an incredibly powerful experience and is truly beneficial to the relationship. We will discuss more about this later.

- **Can Be Confidential:** Remember that trust is critical in any relationship. No one tells you something in confidence that they want you to spread around. Make sure that you're willing to keep the conversation between you and your friend if you're going to let them tell you anything of merit.

- **Know That You Don't Have to Fix the Issue:** No one is expecting you to wave a magic wand and fix everything that is going wrong in your friend's life. Most of the time, your loved one doesn't even want you to. Most of the time, they just want a friendly shoulder to lean on and a pair of listening ears.

Make sure that if you haven't seen each other in a while, whether it's defined as a regular emotional check-in or not, you meet somewhere private so as to not be distracted or disturbed.

How Can I Ask if a Friend is Okay?

You may not be overly emotionally intuitive, or maybe you just have never really asked someone if they were okay and it may feel awkward. There is an art to starting a check-in. Asking closed questions such as "Are you okay?" is really not recommended as that sort of question can quickly be avoided. If you're asking open-ended questions, your friend is likely to give you a deeper response and that will turn into a conversation. Ask them how they're doing at work, or how their significant other or children are doing, etc. These sorts of questions get the ball rolling.

When Should I Check in with Friends?

Check-ins can be prompted by a number of things. For example, maybe you haven't heard from your friend in a while, or maybe something you saw or heard reminded you of them. Maybe you have heard that they are struggling, or that they have just gone through something traumatic, and you are concerned about them. All of these can be genuine reasons to check in on someone. It is recommended to check in on your friends often. Consider doing a regular emotional check-in.

Catch Up and Share Your Own Journey

When you're checking in on your friend, make sure you're taking ample time to truly share your journey with them, too. Both of you knowing what is going on in each other's lives will develop a stronger bond.

Using feedback obtained from your hangouts, an emotional check-in, or even just during your own self-reflection exercises, you can document your own personal development. Journaling is a great way to record feedback and your own reflections. It can provide a glimpse of previous versions of yourself and give greater insight into your personal growth.

Personal growth is an ongoing journey and sharing these moments of realization—even epiphanies—with your loved ones is an exciting and emotionally bonding experience. Discuss your personal experiences, challenges, and lessons learned through self-reflection and check-ins with your friend.

Along the way, support one another's aspirations and encourage continued self-improvement exercises. Then, go on to celebrate milestones in your personal development journey together. By following these guidelines and strategies, you can improve your communication with your friend, whether they are a CD or an MY. Effective communication is the key to understanding, empathy, and building a strong and thriving relationship. Communicating where each of you are and where you hope to be in the future is crucial for understanding one another on a deeper emotional level.

Respect Their Space and Yours

Learning other people's boundaries can take time, and as mentioned earlier in Chapter 2, boundaries need to be revisited throughout the relationship. However, respecting space is a boundary that should always be in place.

Have you ever over-shared with someone, were late when you were supposed to meet them, or messaged someone particularly late at night? Or maybe you've pushed a friend to hang out even though you knew they were tired?

If so, you have likely crossed/violated someone's boundary. Boundaries are in place to protect our emotional, mental, and physical preferences/needs. It's important to respect your friend's space—or boundaries—as well as yours. It's important to:

- **Watch for Non-Verbal Cues:** People don't always communicate when they need space. Watch out for levels of discomfort and make sure you're asking questions—without interrogating—regarding your friend's comfortability and how you might assist. By learning how to pay attention to others' body language, we are able to gauge levels of discomfort.

- **Be Empathetic:** You may not understand someone else's emotions or need for space. Perhaps you're an MY (need little space) and they're a CD (needs a lot of space). Regardless, it's important to put yourself in their shoes or see the world from their lens. Try to be understanding.

- Be Receptive: If someone says or acts like they need space, give it to them. You would want your space respected, so respect theirs.

Apologize When Necessary

Relationships can be wonderful buffers against stress, but conflicts can arise and then turn those relationships into something that brings a considerable amount of emotional pain and/or stress.

Knowing how to apologize—and when you should—is essential in repairing damage to a relationship. Be sure to mean it and to do it effectively, because a poorly executed apology can lead to damaging the relationship more.

Being sincere and communicating with genuine empathy, remorse, or regret are all components of a successful apology. There should also be some sort of promise to learn from your mistakes. However, it is not your sole responsibility to fix your relationship. It's important to know when to apologize and when not to apologize—because after all, you need to mean an apology.

Recognize If You Should Apologize

Most of the time you understand when you've made a mistake or hurt someone. Of course, there are many reasons to apologize if this has occurred. By apologizing, you are able to acknowledge that you were wrong and made a mistake, begin discussing boundaries with your friend again, express regret and/or remorse, are able to learn from your mistakes, and can open up a dialogue with your friend with complete honesty.

However, there are times when you may not need to provide an apology. Understanding and recognizing when to apologize is just as important as knowing how to apologize. Generally speaking, if you suspect that you did something—whether on purpose or by accident—that might have caused someone to be upset, it's a good idea to apologize just to clear the air.

Be empathetic and ask yourself, "If it happened to me, would I be bothered?" If the answer to that is "yes" then you likely should offer an apology.

Apologies give us the opportunity to own our mistakes; but if you feel you didn't make one, consider explaining why what you did was acceptable in your opinion. If you feel, after explaining, that they're being unreasonable, a discussion may be in order. And then you can decide on an apology after you hear their side of things.

Take Responsibility

Apologizing is difficult but it can be humbling. Taking responsibility for mistakes you make is not only essential to keeping a functioning relationship with your friend, but it's also a great way to grow as an individual.

And remember, if you decide that apologies are in order, you should mean it, and be specific and direct. If you say something like, "I am sorry if you were offended by what I did," that implies that their hurt feelings are a random reaction. Instead acknowledge what happened specifically such as "When I did [the thing that upset them], I wasn't thinking. I understand that I hurt you and I am sorry."

Whatever you do, take full responsibility. Don't make assumptions or shift the blame. Make it clear that you regret what happened and that you sincerely apologize.

Express Regret

As mentioned, make sure you're properly expressing your regret. That is one of the keys to learning how to apologize effectively. Taking responsibility for your actions is crucial, sure, but it's even more critical to show that you feel bad about upsetting your friend.

Reaffirm Boundaries

After you apologize, make amends, and reaffirm your boundaries with one another, especially if you crossed them without realizing it. Discussing what type of rules you both will abide by in the future will help rebuild trust and will give you an opportunity to work together in setting future expectations on how you should treat one another.

Don't Bring Up Their Part During Apologies

Remember that when you do decide to apologize, you're taking responsibility for your part of the situation. It doesn't mean that you are admitting complete fault, but it also doesn't mean you point the finger at the other person. Instead, open up the communication dialogue and apologize for your part in it. Show that you regret your actions. It is likely that your friend will also apologize for their part during the conversation; but if they don't, that is on them. Use that opportunity to reassess if they're as committed as you are to your friendship.

Create Open and Honest Dialogue

Effective and open communication is foundational to the long-term success of your friendship. Keep in mind that it may be more difficult for some than others to communicate openly. Get to know your friend and their background, and establish whether having open dialogue is something they're used to. Start with these steps:

- **Agree to Talk:** Agree to talk openly with your friend. Be clear, concise, and honest about everything. This will set the bar. Just make sure that you're having deep conversations in private. You don't want to have outward opinions or input and you certainly don't want distractions. Remember that listening is essential to good communication.

- **Share Emotions**: Agree to support your friend through their varied emotions and allow them to do the same. Bottling up emotions is unhealthy and counterintuitive to open communication. Encourage your friend to speak freely and agree to treat them with respect and patience and reassure them that there's a safe space in your communication for them to be honest and open.

- **Value and Respect Their Opinions:** Keep an open mind and the communication floor completely open, without fear of judgment or argument. This will help everyone stay connected and valued.

Your compassion is essential in maintaining your friendship, as well as helping your friend feel welcome and wanted in your life.

Key Takeaways:

Effective communication forms the foundation of all healthy and flourishing relationships. It goes beyond the confines of personality types, but learning about them can be a great place to start. This chapter has explored how you might engage with your friend on a deeper level and communicate about issues that you may have with them, or the past you have together.

Start difficult discussions by expressing feelings without instigating conflicts. It is important, no matter what happens, to remain calm and collect yourself before delving headfirst into the conversation. Remember, others are a lot more likely to consider your perspective if they feel that they can voice their concerns without you jumping off the deep end or responding out of anger and vice versa. The best ways to express yourself without conflict is to:

- **Express Feelings with Words, Not Actions:** If you feel anger rising to an uncontrollable level, take a step back and return to the conversation after you've calmed down. Consider engaging in other activities that help you regain your composure. Encourage your friend to do the same. Use methods such as walking, deep breathing, or journaling to manage strong emotions constructively.

- **Address One Issue at a Time:** Avoid resorting to the "kitchen sink" approach. Focus on one issue at a time when discussing conflicts.

- **Resist Underhandedness:** Steer clear of using underhanded or hurtful tactics when discussing sensitive topics. Attacking your friend in sensitive areas only fosters distrust, anger, and vulnerability, which is counterproductive to communication.

- **Be Specific and Productive:** When expressing concerns, be specific and avoid making generalized statements using words such as "never" or "always." Broad complaints are challenging to address and usually aren't even true.

Once you can communicate effectively, make sure that you are demonstrating active listening skills during conversations and that you're using neutral language. "I" and "We" statements are best to be employed to emphasize that you are working together for a common goal and that you are not attacking them.

CDs may be a little less vocal during communications, and that's okay! Appreciate the silence. Allow them the space and time to collect their thoughts and feelings. Avoid pressuring them to speak immediately after a conflict, and create a safe environment where silence is just considered a part of the communication process.

MYs on the other hand don't do as well with silence. Make sure that you are offering verbal affirmations to help them feel safe and loved during communication. Compliment them genuinely.

The next thing we learned about is how the dynamic may shift as you grow older and that the relationship you have with your friend evolves as life goes on. Respect this shift and communicate new boundaries or expectations appropriately.

Remember to deal with any issues respectfully and check in with your friend often after you have made time to schedule personal time for reflection.

Chapter Three

Strengthen Your Bonds

Friendships are built on the foundation of shared experiences, mutual understanding, and a sense of appreciation for one another. In this chapter, we delve into various ways to fortify these connections and foster deeper emotional bonds. From offering compliments to engaging in surprise gestures, and cooking together to embarking on adventures, this chapter is a treasure trove of ideas to enrich your friendship.

Give Compliments

We have all complimented someone and also received compliments. There are times that they feel awkward but it's still worth doing. According to leading psychological research, appreciation is a foundation in all relationships. Compliments are a great tool to communicate your appreciation for your friend. Even if it's as small as "I like your outfit," make sure that you're properly communicating your appreciation. MYs particularly love compliments, so if you find that your friend is an MY, make sure that you let the compliments flow! Your CD friend would also like them, just be sure not to bombard them with compliments all at once, since it might feel a bit awkward and overwhelming for them.

Offer Surprise Gestures

Let's face it, the truth of the matter is that people want to stay friends with people who make them feel like they have value. One of the best ways to show that is to be generous in the way of gestures. They don't always have to be grand, but they should show some sort of thought. In fact, studies show that people who exhibit traits such as generosity and empathy are more likely to build long-lasting friendships.

MY personality types tend to gravitate toward surprise gestures more than their CD counterparts, but everyone enjoys feeling special. No matter where your friend may fall in the personality spectrum, it is almost certain that they can appreciate a random surprise gesture!

Cook for Them

Enjoy food and time together. This is a great opportunity to bond and spend quality time with each other and forge a truly healthy dynamic.

Call Them Often

If you are living far away from your friend, or at least far enough that weekly visits are out of the question, make sure you call them as often as you can. Take advantage of all the good that technology can bring and make your friend feel as though you are still close to them even if you're actually far away. Over the call, you can even opt to FaceTime or video call and show them what's new with you rather than just telling them! This can be a great way to spend time with your friend without the need to be physically present.

Go With Them on a Trip

A change of weather and location is a natural way to refresh and rejuvenate. It can also give you a chance to unwind from the monotony of life. Take a small road trip with your friend or invite them on a weekend getaway.

Surprise Them with Gifts

No need to wait on special occasions. Sometimes the best gifts are "just because" gifts. Pampering your friend is a great way to help them feel loved and appreciated. So, schedule a gift delivery to their home or take it to them yourself and make them smile from ear to ear.

Make a Surprise Visit to Them

If you and your friend miss each other and they're a little further away than you'd like, consider making a surprise visit to them! They would love it, and you could both get much-needed bonding time together. Spend the entire weekend with them if you can!

Pamper Them with a Spa Day

Just because they may not be used to the idea, or maybe have never even had one, don't sleep on the fact that a spa day is great for rejuvenating the soul! Sometimes our friends forget to take care of themselves. So, book a spa appointment for them so you can help them to relax and recharge their batteries. Consider booking a couple's spa for them and their partner so that they can spend some cozy time with one another.

Walk Down Memory Lane

Revisiting cherished memories and reliving special moments can be a powerful way to enhance emotional closeness with people. Remember, it doesn't take long to develop lasting memories with someone. So, whether you have been friends all your lives, or it's just a recent development, it's possible that you both have great memories together. It is important to highlight and remember major milestones in your life with them. Some great ways to walk down memory lane include:

- **Looking at Photos Together**: These can be photos from your childhood or from more recent times you have spent together. Look at them together and talk about the experiences you shared.

- **Creating a Memory Jar**: This is a fun activity no matter your age. Each of you should write down your favorite memories together on small sheets of paper and place them in a jar. Go through them periodically together, especially when you're trying to shed some positivity on the friendship.

- **Revisiting Special Places**: These can be places special to each of you individually or special to the two of you together Examples of this would include favorite vacation spots, the place where you first met, your childhood hometowns, a special restaurant, or a favorite theme park.

- **Watching Home Movies:** Pull out old videos of your time together. This can be on a disc, a VHS, or even in digital format. It is recommended to broadcast it to a large screen, if possible, but regardless, make it a nice experience. Create a comfortable sitting environment and get out the popcorn and candy! Have fun with it!

Use Your Skills

Take a good look at yourself. Think about what you could bring to the table as far as skills and talents and how you might turn those into a gesture for your friend. Maybe you have a skill for woodwork, and your friend has been talking about needing a new set of steps or a deck built. Offer your time and expertise for free and help them. Maybe you have a skillset in personal finance and they want investment help. Maybe you're a personal trainer and they need help getting into shape. No matter what kind of skillset or talent you have, share it with your friend and turn it into some sort of gesture or kindness for them.

Hug Them

Not everyone is huge on physical touch or affection. This may seem awkward to you, or even your friend, but on occasion, it may be nice for your friend to receive a hug from you. This doesn't have to be a surprise attack, but instead, just a small token of affection that can ultimately go a long way depending on the friendship. Remember, physical affection isn't just for romantic relationships. It can apply to all meaningful relationships if the time and place are appropriate. Just be cautious and make sure that your friend would appreciate a hug and that your relationship dynamic calls for it in the way of boundaries.

No matter what you do to show your friends that you value them in the way of gestures and generosity, just make sure that you do it! If you're having a difficult time deciding what you can do to show them that you love and appreciate them, never be afraid to ask! A simple "How would you like me to show you have much I value you?" can go a long way! Everyone is different and sometimes all you need to do is ask to ensure you're both on the same page.

Write Them Letters

Talking to your friend about what you are thinking or feeling can sometimes be a challenge, especially if you weren't raised in a household where you expressed yourself vocally. Sometimes it can be beneficial to try to communicate something that is emotional for you by letter instead. This can take pressure off by allowing you the outlet you need to get things off your chest and providing your friend with an opportunity to receive the information in a private space where they can properly process their feelings. Remember, although you can do this to express your feelings on big subject matters you don't want to discuss in person, you can also use this as a way to grow closer emotionally. There need not be an occasion; sending a letter can be a simple way to catch up. Regardless of the subject matter, before beginning make sure you organize your thoughts first. It's important to know what you want to convey to your friend. Remember, too, that you can't take back what you write, and that this is an opportunity to share your feelings without interruption—so be authentic and genuine!

Make New Memories

There was a time when you didn't know your friend. They had a whole life before you, and you had a whole life before them. Even if you met young, you likely still have memories without them. People make new memories all the time, and even if you have had the excellent opportunity of having years and years of memories with your friend, it's still important to make new memories with them.

While revisiting memories or places that are important to you and your past is often an emotional experience, it is still important to make sure you're making new memories together, whether you have a lot with your friend or don't have many at all! As you grow and mature, it's important to keep your relationship going and keep it interesting.

Creating new memories with your friend is a wonderful way to strengthen your relationship. These moments can be cherished for a lifetime and can help you connect on a deeper level. Below are some examples of things you can do to make new memories with old friends.

Travel Together

Exploring new destinations can be a fantastic way to bond with your friend. Whether it's a weekend getaway to a nearby town or an international adventure, traveling together allows you to share unique experiences and create lasting memories. Discovering new cultures, trying different cuisines, and exploring historic sites might be exactly what you both need to feel connected with each other and to get a jumpstart on new memories you can cherish forever.

Go on Outdoor Adventures

Spend time in nature by going on hikes, camping trips, or nature walks. The great outdoors offers plenty of opportunities for bonding, and it's a chance to unplug from technology and enjoy each other's company. Consider kayaking or other on-the-lake adventures to kick it up a notch! If someone hasn't tried it, this experience can be even more enriching and mean even more!

Cook and Bake

Preparing meals together can be a fun and delicious way to create memories. Consider trying to cook up a new recipe or bake homemade goodies. Or even consider making it a game. A cook-off with judges is a great way to get other friends or family involved. It's a win-win. You get quality time and yummy food! And if you're competitive, it may be a chance to really show off!

Attend Cultural Events

Explore your city—or a nearby city—and discover what sort of cultural scenes they have. Many cities have showcases of other cultures at various times throughout the year. Learn about some of these by searching online. You may find concerts, theater performances, art exhibits, or even full-blown cultural festivals that may be a ton of fun. Not only will these events provide their own opportunities to appreciate art and culture, but they can also be great ways to make memories with your friend.

Document the Moments

Sometimes we don't remember everything as it was. Consider taking lots of photos and videos to enhance your memories and give you a tangible piece of the memory to cherish in the future.

Volunteer Together

Giving back to the community by volunteering together is not only a meaningful way to bond but also a chance to make a positive impact on your community. Sharing this experience with your friend can be rewarding and create lasting memories centered around compassion and selflessness.

Delve into Mutual Hobbies

Journeying through life is all about exploration. If you and your friend came into each other's lives when you were younger, you may have quite a bit in common. But whether you have a long history or not, there is still plenty of opportunity to find common ground. There is a world of possibilities to explore. Discovering and trying new things together is a chance to bond over shared interests and passions, whether you know you have them or not. The key to keeping a strong connection with your friend is to continually grow with them. What better way to bring forth some freshness than to find a fun new hobby you can partake in together?

When exploring new activities to try, consider their interests and preferences. You can take turns choosing activities with them ensuring that you each have a say. Be open to trying things you may not have considered before; you might come to find that you enjoy something you never thought you could.

Whether it's trying a new cuisine, taking up a dance class, embarking on a road trip, or learning a new skill, the key is to approach these experiences with an open heart and mind and be willing to embrace the unknown. Know that at the end of the day, even if you don't enjoy the activity, doing something different with your friend is sure to create memories and strengthen your relationship by spending quality time together.

Keep in mind that CDs and MYs may enjoy different activities, but also that it's important for you all to try things even if you don't think you would enjoy them. You might surprise yourselves! To make this part of your regular scheduled dates, consider being the first to suggest it. Start with something you know they will enjoy getting the ball rolling!

If you want to experience a new activity with your CD friend, you could try:

- Starting a book club with them.
- Stretching it out with some yoga, whether at a studio or at home.
- Playing games or doing a puzzle together.
- Gardening together.
- Starting a collection.
- Beer brewing at home.
- Learning how to knit together.

Activities you may want to try with your MY friend include:

- Trying your hand at tie-dying.
- Learning a new language together.
- Cooking together.
- Going to an unknown band's concert.
- Trying a martial arts class.
- Going camping or biking.
- Rock climbing.
- Volunteering at a local soup kitchen.

Bring Them Thoughtful Gifts

The practice of gift-giving is deeply ingrained in human culture and even spans much further back than Western civilization. It is a practice that spans thousands of years and exists in almost all cultures and societies.

Research shows that when we give and receive gifts we release serotonin, dopamine, and oxytocin, which brings forth a positive physiological response that aids in lowering blood pressure, stress, and increasing self-esteem. It's a great way to show your appreciation, boost your friend's spirit, and improve your friendship in general.

Make Your Own Traditions

Some people have a strong foundation in their traditions. Some of these traditions might have derived from your family and others you may have just developed on your own. Whatever the case, traditions truly help us cultivate a connection with others. This is because it gives us the opportunity to have meaningful shared experiences with others.

Whether it's your family member or your best friend, you can establish some sort of tradition. In fact, it may be possible that you're closer to your friends than you are to your family. So why not start a new tradition, such as a game night, an annual Friendsgiving, or a Christmas Eve cocktail party?

You can completely start from scratch, or you each can bring ideas together from your own, already established, traditions.

Express Your Appreciation

Our friendships can have a way of bringing warmth, value, and happiness to our lives. In our toughest moments, they can leave us feeling stronger and satisfied. It is through this strength that we must show the people who make our lives worth living how much we appreciate them. Some great practices in showing your appreciation include:

- Verbal Appreciation: Letting your friends know how much you appreciate them at any given moment is essential. Telling them with your words can give them the reassurance that they need and show that you value their existence in your life. A simple "You're a great friend" or "I'm glad you're here" will go a long way!

- Writing Them Notes: As you're communicating with your friend, it's important to remember that the right words often come more easily in written form. Letters and notes are intimate ways to express your appreciation for your friend and are something that they can cherish forever.

- Giving Gifts: Buying gifts is never mandatory but it is a great way to show your friend that you admire them. It shows that you've thought about them enough to go get something for them. It can even be something as simple as buying them their favorite candy or drink.

- Offering Your Help: Struggles happen to everyone. Our friends, no matter how much they seem well put-together, still have their own season of struggles. By offering a listening ear and a space to feel heard, you are showing your friend that they are valued and loved. If they need help, whether it be someone to talk to, someone to do their chores, or someone to offer advice, it's important that you be that for them.

Be Vulnerable

You might want to become more vulnerable in your friendship, especially if you feel that vulnerability is something that's been lacking. If you feel that you've been struggling to connect with your friend emotionally, consider having a deeper conversation and truly opening up.

Explore Your Fears

Before you rush to share your deepest thoughts and dreams, make sure that you understand what's been holding you back in the first place. Being vulnerable opens us up to rejection and that's often a scary situation to find yourself in.

If you have past trauma with rejection, try to speak with someone on how you might start opening up. It is possible that, with a little trust and patience, you can overcome this.

Recognize Who to Share With

The fact that you're reading this guide means you really care for your friend. But it's important to determine if they're worth opening up to, especially when it comes to sensitive topics. Would they judge you? Would they respect your privacy? Make sure you can trust the friend you talk to before sharing sensitive information.

If your friend tends to gossip or put other people down, it's important to be aware of how this might affect your relationship. Look to share with a friend who shows compassion or empathy for others and a friend who is patient, kind, and emotionally mature. If your friend doesn't fit the bill, consider having a conversation with them about your fears. It's possible that they have this behavior and don't even realize it.

Start Slow

You don't have to share your biggest fears, spill every dream you've ever had, or open up about all of your biggest traumas to be vulnerable. You don't have to go all in at first. In fact, it is recommended that you start slow and ease your way into that kind of relationship. This not only helps set the stage in small steps as to what you hope your friendship to be, but it also keeps your friend from being overwhelmed at once and more able to listen and respond. Expand your comfort zone slowly and remember, your friend may not be good at this sort of thing either.

Sometimes it's a good idea to start these kinds of conversations by sharing smaller, less significant details such as where you like to go on vacation and why, some small or irrational fears you might have, or an embarrassing or funny story from your childhood.

Key Takeaways:

In this chapter, we've learned the importance of showing your friend how much you love and appreciate them. You can show your appreciation in a multitude of ways, all of which will strengthen your relationship at its core. Ways to show your friend you value them include:

- **Giving Them Compliments:** Expressing genuine compliments and gratitude is fundamental in growing bonds with friends. Understanding how different personality types respond to compliments can help tailor your approach.

- **Surprising Them:** Engaging in surprise gestures and creating memories, whether through travel, exploring hobbies, or attending events, cements shared experiences and can deepen your bond.

- **Walking Down Memory Lane Together:** Share your memories together by walking down memory lane. Reminisce and reflect on positive times shared. Don't forget to make new memories, though!

- **Communicating with Them:** Maintaining connections through communication, no matter your distance, is critical. Regular calls, video chats, and letters can bridge the gaps you have between seeing each other in person. This is a great way to foster emotional intimacy without being physically there.

- **Making Your Own Traditions:** Establishing traditions creates a sense of belonging and strengthens the fabric of friendship. Why not bring the best of both of your worlds into one fun tradition that you can maintain over the course of your lives?

- **Being Vulnerable:** Learning to navigate vulnerability is no easy task. Sharing thoughts, fears, and aspirations is scary, but it also allows for a deeper understanding between friends and strengthens emotional connections.

Chapter Four

Celebrate Your Friend

Friendship can be a treasure trove of shared, heartfelt moments. It truly is a journey worth celebrating—and so is your friend. In this chapter, we embark on an intentional voyage of honoring and uplifting our friends through an array of thoughtful gestures and acts.

Invite Them Over for a Friend Night or a Party

In a world dominated by technology, it's easy to forget that your friends are human beings and need in-person social interaction (even the CDs, who are more reserved) every now and again. While group texts, Facebook posts, and emails are easy, make sure you're making that extra effort to invite your friends over for a night of fun.

It can be difficult to get everyone together. As adults, we often hear "let me check my schedule," or something similar as a response, rather than a commitment to attend a party or event. Being a host with this sort of non-commitment can be stressful because it generally means that you're running around near-last-minute to get things done.

Give your guests ample time and let them know any event is not mandatory. But still follow up with them—and give yourself enough time to plan if it's a go or not.

Clearly Communicate Intentions

Make sure you let everyone know why you're throwing this shindig. Is it a birthday? Is it a "just because?" A holiday? Let them know. If you want, even formulate invitations. Be clear and concise in your communication about what the intent is of the party and what is expected during the party (i.e., are you having a meal, exchanging gifts, etc.). Generally, if this is a friend get-together/hangout then you likely don't need to clarify any of that, but if the event has a specific purpose other than getting together, it may be beneficial to clarify.

Be Ready When They Arrive

As a host, it can be a little on the stressful side when your guests arrive and you're still finishing up (whether that be with food, prepping, or getting dressed). Know that human beings generally congregate where the action is, so try to finish up everything before they arrive.

Mix and Mingle with Everyone

It's your job as the host to make sure everyone feels included and has a good time. If you've invited people from other social circles, make sure you're making introductions and keeping the conversation going. This can be a bit of a difficult task, so if you plan on mixing company, be prepared for a bit of extra work.

Remember Important Dates

No matter where you are physically from your friend, make sure that you're still giving your friendship adequate attention and care to keep it in good health. Long-lasting relationships share one characteristic, and that is reciprocity. If both people equally engage and share with one another, the greater the likelihood of a healthy and long-lasting relationship.

With busy schedules, it can seem a little daunting to squeeze in phone calls and write letters. But finding a time that works for both you and your friend will alleviate this pressure, even if it's during your commute to or from work, or right before or after dinner. Whenever works best, try to make sure it happens consistently. And always, always, always remember important dates.

Anniversaries and birthdays in long-distance friendships carry additional weight. Try to put in a little more effort on these sorts of occasions. If you can't be there in person then consider sending flowers, balloons, or a nice card on special occasions. Remember, a little thought and care will go a long way!

Honor Them

At the end of the day, good friends deserve a special place in our lives. In a country where family sizes are growing smaller and the family unit is weakening, friendships are becoming increasingly important. People are marrying later in life and having fewer children, and consequently, friends have a greater role now than they ever have. However, as important as they are, we don't typically depend on our friends or give them the special treatment they always deserve. Some ways you might honor your friends include:

- Being there to help if/when things go wrong.

- Being there to celebrate if/when things go right.

- Being there just to be there!

- Remembering their birthdays or special anniversaries.

- Planning trips with them.

- Considering counseling if something is troubling either (or both) of you.

Share Music with Each Other

We have all shared music with people who mean something to us. Doing this with your friend is a great way to share your feelings or connect.

We are fortunate to live in a world of technology where so much music is at our fingertips. For the majority of human history, the only way to experience music was live. There were no recordings, and there was no way to share—outside of a performance anyway. Take advantage of that privilege and share music from your playlists with your friends!

Music Gives Us an Oxytocin Boost

Oxytocin (known widely as the "love drug") is a neuropeptide and it is known to play an important role in bonding with and trusting people. Research shows that levels are increased with music.

Like Minds

When we discover that someone likes a piece of music that we also like, we tend to think more of them. It is as though as human beings we feel that musical preference holds a deeper meaning than what entertains someone. In fact, studies have shown that people often affiliate musical taste with values and morals. Therefore, it is safe to assume that we feel even more connected to people who have the same music tastes as us. That's not to say that you and your friends don't share values if your music preference differs, but this is one way that you can deepen your relationship if you feel your friend can relate to your song choices.

Having something in common with your friends is, at the end of the day, all that is really sought in a friendship. If that's music, then what a wonderful way to bond! Songs often carry meaning in them, and if each of you can express yourselves through music, and find a common ground in it, then by all means, rock on!

Encourage Self-Care

Self-care is a commitment to yourself. It is a promise to prioritize your well-being when making decisions or going about daily tasks. When we optimize self-care, we feel better, look better, and even have more energy. In fact, quality self-care is to improved mental health, which in turn has benefits such as greater self-esteem, self-worth, and positivity. This leads to lower levels of anxiety and depression.

It can become easy to get wrapped up in the everyday monotony of life and forget to take time for yourself, but you shouldn't let that happen. After all, at the end of the day, we have ourselves longer than we have anyone, and we owe it to ourselves to take care of our minds and bodies.

You also owe it to your friend to make sure that you're encouraging them and their journey of self-care, as well.

Of course, this may or may not be easy, depending on your friend and their personality type. Self-sacrifice is usually well-intended. Generally, people sacrifice their happiness to make others happy. This is over-extending and can lead to a slew of issues.

When you are tired or dissatisfied with something in your life, it's not outside of the realm of possibility that you may grab a quick fix or indulge in habits and/or behaviors that offer distraction rather than solution. This can become a bit of a tiresome loop that you replay over and over again. When engaging in such behavior, your brain becomes fogged, you become fatigued, and you can feel more over-extended than ever.

In times like this, it's important to recenter yourself by pressing pause and redirecting your energy on taking care of yourself; and your friend should do the same. Encourage them to realize that they get to choose how to live their life and that it needs to be in a way that supports both physical and mental health. Ways to encourage your friend to practice self-care include:

- Making sure you are practicing self-care.

- Encourage them to make quality food and get sufficient rest.

- Give them quality time and encourage them afterward to have time to themselves.

- Show them how to be nice to themselves.

- Stay connected and encourage them to make sure that they're taking time to connect with themselves and others.

- Send them a song that they love.

- Take them out for a walk in nature.

- Surprise them with a spa day or something that they can do, either with you or alone, that brings them joy!

- Sit in the sunshine with them!

Practice Inclusion

This is mostly in regard to mixed company. Sometimes we crave for all of our friends to meet and/or get along. However, in group settings, inside jokes and stories often come up. Not everyone at the table is going to understand or get everything that is discussed. To combat this, make sure that you briefly explain what you mean, or bring up something that you experienced with the other people at the table, too. This helps everyone feel included and avoids awkwardness.

Explore Each Other's Neighborhoods

When your friends live far away, staying in touch can be a challenge. Instead of simply texting or calling, try to get to know some things about your friend's neighborhood. This is especially useful when you plan trips to see them.

Share Photos

Share photos of your area with your friend, and even consider making a game out of it! When you visit each other, go to the places where you took the photos to mark the occasion! Photo walks can be a lot of fun and they incorporate exercise with memory stamps.

Make a Book

Every neighborhood has a story of some kind! Do some research on each other's neighborhoods and plan things to do together—or something your friend can do without you in their own neighborhood—and highlight some of the area's history.

Make Coupons

If you are going to visit one another soon, consider making a coupon book of experiences for each of you to cash in when you see one another. Think of parks, museums, dessert places, restaurants, or anywhere that either of you might be excited to go! Cash them in when you want to hit those things up! This gets you guys thinking of bonding experiences together and gives you both something to look forward to.

Grab a Bite to Eat

When you do actually get to hang out with one another, make sure you do everyone's favorite thing—go out to eat. This can be a long-awaited restaurant (like something you made a coupon for previously), somewhere new, or a favorite of each other's! Make it a great experience, and don't always stick to the same place! Ask for local recommendations and make a game out of finding new, and interesting places to eat at!

Go for a Stroll or a Drive

There's no better way to get to know someone's neighborhood than immersing yourself in it. Take in the sights, the smells, the sounds—all that it has to offer, even if it seems small. There are likely hidden gems somewhere that neither of you would have even thought of, and that includes the person who lives there!

Pretend You Are Both Tourists

Whether you meet in your neighborhood or your friend's, treat the experience as if you were both tourists. This is the best way to find new and interesting spots that neither of you would have thought about previously. What is your neighborhood known for? Have you seen all the museums? Do a quick search online to find something you haven't done, or just hit the pavement and start exploring first-hand.

Shop Local

Almost all towns/cities have chain stores. But instead of hitting them up, while you're out exploring, find some shops that catch your eye and make it a point to visit them! Shopping local can be a great way to explore, but it also gives you a unique shopping experience that you wouldn't have received at a mainstream store. It also supports local people, which is a great way to support your neighborhood in all its glory.

Get Involved in Community Events

What better way to get to know your area than to check out local events? Maybe there's a play coming up, or a gala, or even a festival! Check out all of your local organizations and see what there is to offer. A lot of towns/cities do festivals around holidays or season changes. Spring, Summer, Fall, Halloween, Christmas, etc.—they generally always have festivals and events happening around them. Meet local shops and vendors by going to these and exploring more of what your neighborhood and others nearby have to offer! Check out the Chamber of Commerce, too! They usually have a lot of great events that you can attend completely for free.

Share in Their Joys

Do you get super excited when your friend succeeds? Do you love to see their face light up? If so, then you enjoy sharing their joy, and this is a crucial part of making a friendship work. You can share joy in some of life's most exciting moments, or in the small, insignificant ones. Ways that you can share in each other's joy can be through recommending a favorite restaurant, sharing a favorite book, or inviting your friend to learn something interesting that you just learned.

By inviting people to share in our joys, we set the stage to share in theirs. You can improve the lives of others by sharing new things with them that they may enjoy, too. This allows you to have your joy enhanced and/or validated because someone else enjoyed the same thing you did.

Respect Their Time

In today's world, time is a currency. We don't have nearly enough of it, and everyone wants it. But here's the thing—it's also the one commodity in which we cannot make more. However, when it comes to our loved ones, it's essential. There are some creative ways we can maximize the use of our time, but generally speaking, understand that—like you—your friends have a finite amount of time If someone gives it to you, appreciate it. It is, after all, their most precious gift.

How To Respect Time

The first thing is to do what you say and say what you mean. Of course, it is human nature to want to be liked. This is why we can—at times—jump the gun and say what we think someone wants to hear instead of what is actually the truth. This includes telling them that something is going to happen at a faster timeframe than it is, or that you can do something by a certain time that you know you can't.

Respect starts with honesty. If you can't do that project or can't help someone with something by the time you tell them you will/can, it will create disappointment and more issues in the long run. Think about it, another person is waiting on you to deliver on something, and if you don't deliver, it wastes their time. We have already established that time is precious, so do not take it for granted.

If you find yourself overcommitted, behind on something, or simply not interested in actually doing something in the first place, start by being honest from the jump. Not meeting someone's expectations and telling them upfront is far better than stringing them along.

Communicate Changes as Soon as You Can

There are times that life throws you curveballs. These can't be helped. Accepting and understanding changes is all part of life. Make sure you communicate when something changes in your schedule. If you have promised your friend that you're going to help them with something or do something for them and you have a curve ball thrown at you, make sure you let them know. After all, it is rarely the event that occurs that upsets someone—it's usually being left in the dark until the last minute.

This is another way to truly respect your friend's time. This idea is built on the foundation that you understand and respect the fact that you are not the most important person/thing in someone's life.

Surprise Them

Think of how your friend shows happiness or think of something that genuinely makes them happy. Think about their personality type—CD or MY—and think of ideas of how you might surprise them. One friend might love a surprise trip or experience out, but another would prefer a nice gift and a quiet evening at home. Think about what your friend does for fun, and you'll have a great idea of how to surprise them!

There are multiple ways you can surprise your friend. The surprise could come in the form of a gift, an outing, or just spending quality time together. Figure out what your friend needs or wants. Is there a special treat they enjoy that they haven't had in a while? Are they super stressed and could benefit from a spa day? Try to plan a surprise that's related to your friend's hobbies or needs. If their favorite band is coming to town, consider buying tickets so that the two of you can go to the concert together. If they've had a tough day at work and you know they have a sweet tooth, go get a box of cookies and enjoy them together while you binge-watch your favorite show. Whatever the case, cater the surprise to your friend. It doesn't have to be grand! Just make sure it's something they enjoy.

Key Takeaways:

Celebrating your friend and the friendship you share involves a large spectrum of intentional actions and thoughtful gestures. From hosting dedicated friends' nights to commemorating important milestones, such as birthdays and achievements, each and every gesture underscores the level of appreciation you have for your friend.

It is important to embrace your friend's uniqueness, as well as their strengths, in order to properly celebrate them and truly journey through life, celebrating them and exploring the world together. You can do this by sharing joys, including delving into neighborhood gems together, experiencing each other's music, or recommending restaurants. All of your shared experiences and shared joy contribute to a celebration of your friendship, and this fosters true understanding and respect.

Remember that with understanding and respect comes respect for your friend's time as well. Understand that their time is their most precious gift/commodity. By doing this you grow your trust and the bond the two of you have and ensure that it can be cherished for the rest of your lives.

And finally, embrace and celebrate their individuality. You love them for who they are—a very special and important friend that you clearly hold dear.

Chapter Five

Appreciate Them for Who They Are

In this chapter, we discuss not only accepting but appreciating our friends for who they are—their authentic selves. Life is—and has always been—a journey of discovery, learning, and celebration. Within the pages of this chapter, we uncover the profound value in celebrating our friends' emotional strengths—their resilience, compassion, and unwavering support—and what truly makes them who they are.

Celebrate Their Emotional Strengths

Celebrating the emotional strengths each person brings to the relationship table is essential for bonding and growth. To love your friend more effectively, connect with them emotionally and understand that they have their own emotional gifts.

Identify Emotional Strengths and Compliment Them

Take the time to identify and acknowledge the unique emotional strengths each of you has. CDs often bring introspection, empathy, and stability, while MYs may contribute enthusiasm, spontaneity, and optimism.

Recognize how your emotional strengths complement your friend's and vice versa.

CDs can provide a stabilizing presence during challenging times, while MYs can infuse energy and positivity into the mix where negativity could normally take over. are part of people's identity. Learn to appreciate these differences because they often come with strengths that you may not possess.

Your friend having different emotional strengths than you is actually quite a good thing, as it can lead to friendships strengthening over time. This is because each of you can feed off the other's energy. Where one person lacks, the others can cover the bill, and vice versa.

Express Gratitude

Regularly express your gratitude for your friend and the emotional strengths they can bring to the table. If you've had a particularly bad day and your MY friend has supported you and provided a fresh, upbeat, and optimistic breath of fresh air into your lungs, make sure you acknowledge that and express your gratitude to them. Perhaps you feel like your life has found its way rolling down a tumultuous road, and they bring stability where you don't feel it anywhere else. Let them know how their qualities have positively impacted you. A simple "Thank you" can go a long way.

Understand That They're Human—Just Like You

As we discussed in this guide, a funny thing happens when you become an adult. You finally start to realize that the world doesn't revolve around you and that human beings are all flawed. Your friends make mistakes, just as you do, and you have to understand that you must set your expectations for them to a realistic standard. You also need to hold your relationship with your friend to a realistic standard. Nurturing your bond every single day is important, but it isn't very realistic the older we get. As life's obligations pile up, loving your friend can quickly fall to the bottom of the to-do list. This is okay!

Make sure that you're picking back up as often as you can, and still communicating and expressing your love for one another. It doesn't have to entail grandeur or extravagance. Sometimes it can be a small text message that says, "Thinking of you."

Prioritizing time together—truly quality time—will ensure that your friend feels heard, understood, accepted, and loved. Mix that with small acts or gestures of surprise and kindness and you can truly build a strong foundation that won't be harmed by a missed day (or thirty) of communication.

Learn About Their Story

Everyone has a past. Everyone has a future. Make sure that you're taking time to understand your friend better by asking them about their past. Asking about their experiences can help give you a glimpse of how they have arrived at becoming the person that they are today. We all have different backgrounds and stories. Seek to understand your friends in order to see things from their perspective.

Encourage Their Future Aspirations

Encouraging a friend's aspirations is the same thing as embracing your friend's dreams. If you know their aspirations and dreams for the future, it is likely they have been vulnerable enough to share them with you. By encouraging and supporting them to achieve these successes, your friendship will be immensely rewarded. At the end of the day, encouraging your friend is an incredible gift that not only supports their growth but also strengthens your bond as friends. Your support can be the catalyst that helps them achieve their dreams—and how rewarding is that?

It's important to note that every person harbors dreams, ambitions, and aspirations, and as a friend, you have the power to uplift and support them. Here's how you can effectively nurture your friend's future dreams:

Listen!

As mentioned in the second chapter, you must listen first and foremost. If you start by actively listening to your friend, you will have a better understanding of their exact goals, dreams, and what it is that they're passionate about. Remember, it likely took a lot for them to express these ideas to you. People often hesitate to talk about vulnerable topics such as these for fear of judgment or lack of support. By showing a genuine interest in what your friend has to say and actively asking thoughtful questions, they will almost immediately feel supported.

Provide Supportive Feedback

Offer constructive and supportive feedback when your friend shares their dreams or future aspirations with you. Positively acknowledge their strengths and the effort they've put into their goals so far. If they're seeking advice or guidance, provide it respectfully and without imposing your opinions in a way that crosses a boundary.

Advocate for Them

Act as their advocate. Encourage them during challenging times and celebrate their achievements, no matter how small. And when given the opportunity, advocate for them and let people know why they deserve to have their potential realized. Your enthusiasm and encouragement can provide the necessary motivation for them to keep moving forward.

Help Them Set Realistic Goals

Sometimes when we have our heads in the clouds, it's easy to lose sight of what is real and what is fantasy. Help your friend in setting realistic goals, both short-term and long-term. Make sure that you are respectful when doing this, and don't be a dream crusher. It's important to break down goals into manageable steps and encourage them to create an action plan with achievable milestones. You can help them with this. By doing so, it is quite possible that they are able to see an even clearer path to their dreams.

Offer Resources and Connections

If you have resources to help them along the way, by all means, share them! Even better, if you have a colleague or another connection that you know—or know of—then pass the information about your friend along. You can help them whether it's recommending books, courses, workshops, or introducing them to someone in a relevant position to help them in their quest. No matter what, assisting them with this can impact their journey by not only giving them new information but also showing that you care enough to provide aid.

Provide Emotional Support

Pursuing your dreams often involves facing challenges and setbacks. Be there for your friend emotionally, especially if they hit a snag. Offer a listening ear, provide comfort during tough times, and remind them of their capabilities when self-doubt creeps in.

Encourage Self-Belief

By helping your friend understand their worth, you instill an understanding of confidence in them and their abilities. Remind them of their strengths and past achievements when they feel discouraged. Encourage a positive mindset and help them overcome self-limiting beliefs. They can do this! You believe it—so make sure they do, too!

Respect Their Choices

Sometimes your friend's goals don't always align with your own. If that's the case, make sure that you're still supporting them in their pursuit of what truly makes them feel happy and fulfilled. Remember, everyone's dreams are unique and personal. The fact that they have shared what they want with you means that they trust you. Don't break that bond just because you might disagree with their choices.

Lead by Example

Lead by example by actively pursuing your own aspirations. Be positive in your own journey and your friend is sure to follow. Share your experiences and how you overcome obstacles, especially when they struggle with their own. Your dedication and perseverance can serve as inspiration for your friend, and it can also help you feel rejuvenated to continue to chase your passions, too.

Patience and Consistency

Encouraging someone's dreams is an ongoing process that requires patience and consistency. If you're feeling discouraged, they'll pick that up. And if you feel impatient, think of how they might be feeling. Be there for your friend consistently, through both successes and failures, and remind them that no matter what, they are worthy—and loved.

Celebrate Their Uniqueness

We all know that everyone is their own person. We are all made up of our own unique experiences and interactions, and that, coupled with our personalities, is what makes us all unique to every person we meet. Realizing that there is no one else out there who can be quite like you is a little cool if you think about it.

It's almost as if every person in the world is like a colorful puzzle piece that fits perfectly and makes up one piece of the world. No puzzle piece is the same. We are all unique, but all form together to create the human race. It's neat. It's romantic. And it's time we recognize and celebrate one another for that uniqueness.

Unique Talents and Abilities

Just like everything else, we all have our own ways to express our uniqueness. These usually come in the form of our own unique skills, abilities, or talents.

You've met people who can sing like angles, and then other people who can build almost anything you ask them to. You've seen painters, chefs, and writers. All of these people have their own unique talents and abilities. So do you—and so does your friend. Embrace those talents, put them into action, and find a way to impact those around you.

Unique Perspectives and Experiences

We are unique not only because of our abilities but because of our perspectives and experiences.

No two people have lived the exact same life; not even siblings or twins. And that's what makes human beings so fascinating. Each of us has our own past experiences that have helped shape us into who we are today. Celebrate the fact that your friend has experiences that you don't have. Celebrate that they are their own, unique person who you have grown to love and appreciate. Sharing our perspectives with others will help broaden each other's understanding of how we see the world by looking at it through another lens. But celebrate yourself—and your friend—for each having your own set of glasses that views the world in different, unique, and interesting ways.

Accepting and Embracing Your Differences

When it comes to defining your uniqueness and understanding that others are different, there is a final piece of the puzzle that is a little more challenging. You may understand that someone is unique and has a different perspective or ideology from you—but it's another thing to accept and even embrace that difference. However, it is a crucial part of truly accepting your friend for who they are.

Remember that each of us is a mosaic. We all carry different strengths, weaknesses, and quirks that shape our individuality. It's important to note that your friend's differences are not shortcomings. They have a great perspective that, with a little empathy and understanding, you can easily become a part of. Celebrate it and appreciate your friend—just as they should celebrate and appreciate you.

Key Takeaways:

Appreciating our friends for who they are involves celebrating their uniqueness, including their own individual emotional strengths. Where one person lacks, the others can supplement and cover the bill, and vice versa.

Having a friendship means not only acknowledging all the good your friend does for you but also respecting their flaws and taking them completely as they are. A great way to show your friend your appreciation is by:

- **Meeting Them Where They Are:** Understand that your friend is human—just like you. They are flawed and make mistakes. Give them the benefit of the doubt and make sure to have time for them regardless of what stage in their life they are at.

- **Taking Time to Truly Learn About Their Story:** This aids in gaining empathy to understand different perspectives from your friend.

- **Encouraging Their Future Aspirations:** Nothing shows someone that you are worthy of their trust more than supporting them in their dreams. It is likely that your friend has trusted you enough to be vulnerable with you. By supporting them in their dreams, you are showing them that you care about their future, their goals, and overall, that you care enough about their vulnerabilities not to judge—but rather, support them.

Ultimately, this chapter underscores the importance of cherishing the uniqueness, strengths, and individuality that your friend brings into your life. By doing this you are able to foster a genuine connection rooted in authentic appreciation and understanding.

Chapter Six

Friendship Fences

In this chapter we delve into boundaries, or, as they are referred to in this chapter, "fences." Friendship, much like a garden, requires tender care, attention, and sometimes, the nurturing presence of fences—boundaries—that define and safeguard the integrity of the relationship. In this chapter, we embark on an exploration of maintaining healthy boundaries within our friendships and why those boundaries exist and are critical to the success of friendships.

Set Appropriate Boundaries as Your Friendship Evolves

As we touched on in the second chapter we learned that boundaries are "fences" or "lines" that are critical to maintaining a healthy friendship. Setting these boundaries is an act that paves the way for understanding and respect.

Friendships can be some of the most rewarding and important relationships in a person's life. Our friends often help us figure out who we are, and they're there for us when things are difficult. They also share our joys and successes. However, there are times when your friendship dynamics change, or when each of you evolves—whether together or independently of one another.

This chapter will review what healthy boundaries in friendship are, why boundaries are necessary, and practical tips for how to set them and continue to change them as your relationship grows and/or changes.

What are Healthy Boundaries in A Friendship?

If you're reading this guide, it's likely that you have a friend who plays a critical role in your life. Perhaps you have had this friend since your teenage years, or even your early adult years when you were first figuring out who you are and who you want to become. Perhaps you're still in that stage and you have yet to see the friendship dynamic changing. If this is the case, understand that no matter what—the dynamic *will* change.

No matter if your friendship with this person feels like the most permanent relationship in your life or not, boundaries are still required for the relationship to remain strong and healthy through all of life's changes.

Learn to Say No

If you're a "yes" person, that's great. However, learning how to say "no" is critical. Saying "yes" continually in a friendship can lead to you feeling overwhelmed and burnt out. This can be detrimental to your friendship as you may start to resent them in the future. You don't have to say "no" all the time, especially if you're a people-pleaser, but consider mixing it in from time to time. Remember, a true friend will leave space for you to give yourself a little self-care. A "no" will never compromise a healthy friendship.

Redirect

Difficult conversations have to happen sometimes. Boundary setting can be a particularly challenging conversation; so much so that you don't want to do it more than once if you can help it. Communicating your boundaries effectively the first time can curb the need to redirect. Sometimes, however, it can be necessary to change or redirect your boundaries. For instance, if you have set a boundary in which you would prefer your friend not to complain about someone else the two of you know and they do anyway, try to redirect the conversation. Instead of yelling at them for crossing your boundary, attempt to redirect them. Simply saying something like "I'm sorry everything is difficult between the two of you, but let's talk about something else." This can typically give them enough insight to understand that you're not interested in continuing the conversation. If they press further, stand your ground and be even more stern.

Ask If You Have Been Too Needy

There are times when you might have used your friend's shoulder a few too many times in a short period of time. Remember, your friend is also human. They can only take so much before they become overwhelmed and burdened themselves. You never want to be emotionally draining to your friend. And vice versa, don't let your friend become emotionally draining to you. Make sure the two of you are communicating effectively. Be supportive and kind to one another but remember, both of you have your own gauges for emotions. Communication of your limits with one another is essential in maintaining a healthy relationship.

Don't Be Afraid to Ask for What You Need

People aren't mind readers. No matter how much your friend knows you, they won't know exactly what you need unless you ask for it. A really useful skill in life is finding ways to state a need in a respectful way. In fact, this is a tool that will benefit you across all relationships, which includes friendships, romantic relationships, and even your professional ones. Letting people know what you need (such as solidarity or space) allows people the chance to respect that request. Without your communication, they might not have the ability to realize your needs and preferences and may overwhelm you without meaning to. By communicating your need for solidarity/space, you can successfully avoid conflict or hard feelings.

Validate and Reaffirm Your Friend

When you first have a "boundary" discussion with your friend, it can be truly difficult. It's easy to worry that your friend will be hurt, but it's important to understand that there are ways to improve everyone's experience during this conversation. By practicing open dialogue with your friend, you will be able to develop a sense of how to express yourself to them positively. Reaffirm your friendship with them and what they do right and/or what you enjoy about them. MYs are especially fond of this sort of treatment. Telling them that you enjoy being their friend, and letting them know why, can really reinforce that trust, and that in turn makes the conversation a lot more palatable.

Be Direct

Some people may have difficulty with this at first, but it truly is the best policy. Skirting around a subject can often lead to misunderstandings and confusion. Clarity really helps others understand where you are and what you need. They need to understand where they stand with you. At the end of the day, any uncertainty in a friendship can cause hurt. Besides, your friend is likely to be more perceptive in hearing something from you in a direct manner, rather than upsetting you later and not knowing why. So, be direct when asking for what you need! You can be kind and respectful and still clear as glass!

Ask for Advice and Listen When They Give It

While you can set boundaries for your friends and vice versa, it's important to note during your boundary discussion the importance of respecting one another's advice as well. For example, if you're going to ask your friend for advice, don't ignore them when they give it to you. Doing so shows you don't respect them or their time. Going to them for advice may seem like second nature at this point, but it shouldn't be taken for granted. Or, on the flip side, it may sound absolutely horrifying to you to ask them for advice; and in that case, why would you put yourself through a difficult situation only to not listen to or take the advice seriously? Either way, your friend will feel important and trusted if you go to them for advice every once in a while, and if they give you that advice, make sure you're taking proper care to heed it—or at the very least, thank them for it if you take a different route.

Respect Differences

In chapter five we discussed the importance of uniqueness and individuality. When you set boundaries in your friendship, it's important to note that there will be differences in opinion. Part of celebrating your friend for their uniqueness is to understand and respect the fact that there are differences between the two of you.

You may have one boundary for yourself for your friend to abide by, and they may request something completely different from you. While it's normal to wish that others were different than they are, and you may wish that your friend was more like you in certain situations, it's important to always have respect for each other's differences. It is also okay to try to influence them in positive ways and to debate subjects as you see fit, but it is not okay to disrespect another person's perspective. Issues arise when people become self-righteous, angry, or condescending. That is when a situation becomes toxic and potentially abusive.

Diversity can be an absolutely wonderful thing as it makes the world a much more interesting place. Respect your friend's differences, even if those differences can sometimes butt against yours and become frustrating.

Don't Forget "You Time"

In the same boat as self-care is "you time." Giving yourself proper "you" time is essential in setting friendship boundaries. It's all a balance, and although it's admirable to give your whole self to your friends and family, it's often necessary to take a step back to recharge those batteries and do something only for you. "You time" serves as the sanctuary for self-reflection, personal growth, and rejuvenation. It's a deliberate pause—a moment that you can take in order to indulge in activities that bring you joy and fulfillment, as well as recharge your spirit.

Whether it's pursuing hobbies or engaging in solitary activities at home in your pajamas, this time is essential as it carves out space for valuable self-care and personal introspection.

Prioritizing "you" time not only revitalizes your energy but also allows you to be a more enriching and authentic presence in your friendships. How can you be one hundred percent for your friends if you aren't one hundred percent for yourself? This intentional investment in your own personal well-being reinforces a healthier approach to relationships and ensures that while you nurture yourself, you in turn nurture the connection between you and your friends.

Be Consistent

Consistency in your boundaries keeps your friendship expectations clear and focused. It is critical that once you've communicated your boundaries you remain steadfast in upholding them. Consistency involves honoring your limits regardless of circumstances or external pressures. Don't let someone make you feel guilty for your boundaries. In fact, boundaries are an essential part of a relationship and end up creating a healthy atmosphere for love to prosper. It's crucial to stand by your decisions to maintain respect for your own needs. This fosters a mutually respectful relationship.

It is important that you consistently reinforce your boundaries when necessary. If a friend unknowingly crosses a boundary, gently remind them. Clear and respectful communication reaffirms the importance of these boundaries and helps maintain understanding.

Set Consequences (If Needed)

In situations where boundaries are repeatedly ignored or violated, establish consequences. This doesn't mean immediately ending the friendship, but it might involve reducing interaction or taking a break to reassess the relationship's dynamics. Be communicative if this process ends up needing to happen with your friend.

Prioritize Self-Care

By being consistent in your boundaries, you're also practicing self-care. By focusing on your well-being and not compromising your mental, emotional, or physical health for the sake of avoiding conflict or maintaining a friendship that doesn't respect your limits, you are giving yourself proper care and love. This will only make you a more engaged and better friend, too.

Show Them How to Behave

If boundaries are new with your friend, make sure that your behavior aligns with the boundaries you have set for them. You have to show yourself—and them—the same level of respect. For example, if the boundary is about respecting your time, make sure that you respect your own time by not allowing it to be infringed upon. If they're late to leave for a movie, leave without them. Likewise, model that behavior by respecting their time. Don't be late for their plans if you're asking them not to be late for yours.

Seek Support (If Necessary)

If maintaining boundaries becomes challenging or overwhelming, seek support from trusted individuals, such as other friends, a therapist, or a support group. They can provide guidance and encouragement. If you're seeking out support from a non-professional, make sure that you're not gossiping about your friend. This can lead to hurt feelings and a lot more conflict than has already transpired.

Reflect and Adjust When Needed

Periodically reflect on your boundaries and their effectiveness. Assess whether they're serving their purpose in the friendship. Are you happy? Are they? If necessary, adjust your boundaries based on evolving circumstances or changes in your needs. Make sure that you're asking your friend for their input as well. This will help them feel more like a partner in this journey rather than someone abiding by your rules and your rules only.

Celebrate Progress

Acknowledge and celebrate your consistency in upholding boundaries as well as your friend respecting them. Recognize the positive impact it has on your well-being and the health of your friendship. Celebrating small victories encourages continued commitment on both of your parts.

Maintain Open Communication

Consistency doesn't mean rigidity. Be open to discussing your boundaries if circumstances change or if there's a need for adjustment. Maintaining open lines of communication allows for a better understanding between the two of you. As stated earlier, ask for feedback and make sure that both of you are communicating evenly so that you can both work, mutually, on your relationship.

Practice Patience

Consistency in boundary setting takes time and effort. It can be incredibly draining because it is a continuous process. However, although it is rigorous and might face challenges, it's worth it in the end if your relationship comes out stronger. Be patient with yourself and with your friend as you both navigate these boundaries together.

Key Takeaways:

Navigating the intricate landscape of friendships requires a delicate balance of setting boundaries, seeking advice, respecting differences, and embracing personal space, whether that be yours or your friend's. Setting appropriate boundaries is crucial to your relationship because it:

- **Gives a Sense of Security:** Just as children, when we are given a set of parameters to follow to not "get in trouble" we feel safer and more secure. The same principle applies to boundaries in relationships. Having clear expectations and boundaries from the beginning is a great way to set your friendship up for success.

- **Fosters Mutual Respect**: Although each of you may have your own differences, it's important to respect each other's perspectives and boundaries. By setting them, you're able to gain a greater understanding of your friend and their needs and learn to respect them on a whole new level.

When you find you and your friend struggling with boundaries, it's important to:

- **Prioritize "You" Time:** Self-care is a big part of boundaries because it has to do with your self-worth. Ensuring that you are properly taken care of and prioritized ensures that you have what is best for you and your mental well-being at the forefront of your mind. You cannot be one hundred percent for someone else if you aren't one hundred percent for yourself. Make sure that you're prioritizing "you" time as well as what you want, and don't feel guilty or be afraid to be stern about your wants/needs.

- **Be Consistent and Consider Setting Consequences:** If your friend consistently crosses boundaries, consider setting consequences.

- **Seek Help Elsewhere:** If you feel that you and your friend are struggling to maintain balance in your boundaries, consider seeking advice/help from another source. Just remember, don't gossip about your friend. The goal is to help the relationship, not hurt it.

Chapter Seven
Social Time

This chapter focuses on the social aspect of our relationships and how socialization is needed in every relationship, no matter your personality type. In fact, human beings are quite social creatures. Even if it isn't in your personality to be a social butterfly, it's still a crucial part of your physical and mental development. In this chapter, we delve into the art of socializing with our friends and understanding all the ways that we can love them.

Exercise Together

Exercise has its health benefits. We all know this. You have likely been bludgeoned by it every January-February of your entire life as New Year's resolutions come into the limelight like the Kool-Aid man crashing through a brick wall. However, exercising truly does have magnificent health benefits, and doing it with a friend has been found to be one of the best ways to engage in it!

We all know that exercise is great for our minds and bodies, but at times it can be challenging to maintain an interest that keeps you going consistently. And we all know that with health, consistency is key. Your friend can really aid in a journey to better health, and you can do the same for them. Reasons why exercising with your friend is so beneficial:

- **More Fun:** You are a lot less likely to get bored or stop mid-workout when you have a workout buddy, especially a friend that you love and enjoy spending time with. While you're catching up, having a laugh, and encouraging each other, you are also getting healthier. Consider chatting it up with a friend during exercise and breaks as it can help time pass quickly. Before you know it you will have completed an intense regimen that didn't even feel like work! This can especially be true in a game of squash, tennis, or one-on-one basketball! Play and have fun getting healthy together.

- **You're More Likely to Stick to It:** If you've arranged to meet a friend for a walk or booked an exercise class, you're more likely to keep that commitment than if you were to go it alone. Not wanting to let your friend or exercise partner down can be a great motivator to show up. And as your exercise becomes routine, you'll both find it less challenging and will be more likely to stick to it. Keep in mind that on those days when you don't feel like exercising, a pep talk from your workout buddy might be just the lift you need. Accountability is a great tool in keeping you motivated.

- **You're More Likely to Succeed in Your Goal:** Having someone to motivate you can make all the difference to achieving your goal, whether that goal is spending more time with your friend or achieving peak physical fitness.

- **You'll Work Harder with Someone Else Around:** When you exercise with a friend who's around the same fitness level as you, you're more likely to encourage each other and to push a little harder than you might do on your own. In fact, a friend can bring out your competitive side and cheer you on. Just as you're ready to give up, the sight of your friend powering on and through might be just the motivation you need to keep going.

- **It Can Be More Affordable:** If you decide to hire a personal trainer or even buy certain equipment, splitting the cost between the two of you may save money.

- **Your Friend May Have New Exercise Ideas:** Different perspectives are what make friendships really work and also what makes them enjoyable. It's possible that working out with your friend will give you an advantage in the sense that your workout buddy might have some skills and knowledge that you don't; just as you may have some skills and knowledge that they don't. By working together, you can join forces and come up with new and exciting ways to exercise together.

- **It's Safer:** Having someone to spot you when you're lifting weights or to go running with you, especially when it's dark, means that you have someone to help if something goes wrong.

Let Them Confide in You

Being a trustworthy confidant to your friend is a crucial aspect of building and maintaining a healthy and strong friendship. It's about creating a safe space where your friend feels heard, understood, and supported. By actively listening, maintaining confidentiality, and offering your support, you create a bond based on trust and mutual respect that can withstand the tests of time.

In a friendship, being a trusted confidant is a privilege and it matters because it:

- Strengthens Trust: When your friend confides in you, it indicates a deep level of trust. It solidifies your friendship and creates a stronger, more intimate connection.

- Provides Emotional Support: Offering a safe space for your friend to share their thoughts and feelings allows them to seek emotional support during challenging times.

- Creates Mutual Respect: Being a confidant demonstrates mutual respect in the relationship. It shows that you value their trust and are willing to reciprocate by offering a listening ear; and not only a listening ear, but a safe, judgment-free space in complete confidence.

If you have never been a confidant before, make sure that you maintain the level of trust that your friend has given you by being vulnerable yourself. Consider these steps in being a better confidant:

- **Create a Safe Environment:** Make sure the two of you are alone and the space is free of distractions.

- **Encourage Open Communication**: Do this by being approachable and non-judgmental. Let your friend know that you're available to listen whenever they need to talk and that they can start wherever they like. You can ask open-ended questions to get this started, but don't pry.

- **Practice Active Listening:** Active listening is discussed often in this guide and it's because it is truly one of the most crucial points in the communication phase. If your friend finally confides in you, it is absolutely essential that you practice active listening. Pay attention to their words, emotions, and body language. Provide your full attention without interrupting.

- **Maintain Confidentiality:** Respect your friend's trust by keeping what they told you confidential. Avoid sharing their personal information without their explicit permission.

- **Avoid Judgment:** Create a judgment-free zone where your friend feels safe expressing themselves without fear of criticism or ridicule. Be the friend that you would want at that moment.

- **Be Approachable:** Show genuine interest in your friend's life and well-being. Be approachable and create opportunities for open conversations.

- **Offer Support:** Let your friend know that you're there for them. Offer your support and reassure them that you're willing to listen to whatever they need to say and reiterate that you will not pass judgment.

- **Share Your Own Vulnerabilities:** Sometimes, sharing your own vulnerabilities can encourage your friend to open up even more. It creates a sense of trust and reciprocity in confiding. Just make sure it's something you're ready for.

Have Inside Jokes

Inside jokes are the secret language of friendship, a special code that only you and your friend can understand. It almost feels like the two of you have created a new language, that no one else has ever heard of. While they're generally a little childish, they typically hold a unique power to strengthen bonds by evoking laughter and creating a sense of camaraderie that's exclusive to your relationship. In fact, inside jokes can benefit your relationship by creating:

- **Cultivate Shared Experiences:** Anything can become an inside joke. However, they are generally derived after something happened during an activity or adventure together. The joke is a reminder that you experienced something special together, but it's important to note that you should continue to have shared experiences together in the future. You never know how many inside jokes you could develop as time goes on.

- **Are Playful with One Another:** Allowing inside jokes to naturally emerge from funny situations or conversations is a great way to be playful with one another and simply have fun. Embrace spontaneity and humor in all of your interactions and make sure that you continue to spread light and joy to your friend. They may need it more than you realize.

- **Encourage Exclusivity:** While it's generally more agreeable to be "inclusive" rather than "exclusive," if you're looking at growing the bond in one specific relationship, that call can be completely up to you. You can share inside jokes openly, and you can certainly welcome others into the fold. Think of it as a special and secret club. If you want to explain the joke, you can, but if you don't want to, you don't have to. You and your friend have the right to make that call. It can be something just for the two of you if you would prefer it to remain an "inside" joke and more private in nature.

- **Are Personal:** Inside jokes are like secret treasures, personalized to your friendship, and they showcase the uniqueness of your bond together. Even if you did share it with others, it may be possible it was a "had to be there" situation, or that others might not get your humor directly. That is perfectly okay. Just enjoy the joke with your friend.

- **Strengthen Trust:** Referencing an inside joke signifies trust and closeness because it reiterates the fact that the two of you have something special in the first place. It also shows that at some point in your relationship, you had created an environment where you both felt comfortable and understood. That is an invaluable experience to have in a friendship.

- **Are Timeless:** Inside jokes have a timeless quality. They can resurface after years and still evoke the same laughter and warmth as they did the very first time they were told.

Try New Restaurants Together

Trying new restaurants with your friend, if you're both foodies, may seem like a no-brainer. But if you're not a foodie, it still may be beneficial! Studies show that a great way to cultivate healthy eating habits is to spend more time eating meals, rather than less. In a world always on the go, it can be difficult to take a pause and go back to your roots. Maybe you have kids that are tugging you in twenty different directions, or you have three meetings back-to-back and the only food you're going to get in you in the next few hours is whatever you can munch on on your way to the bathroom. However, research shows that dining with friends and family is not only a valuable way to spend time together but is also much healthier for you.

In fact, eating together releases positive emotions. There really is a reason that humans have been sharing meals together since the beginning of time. We are social creatures, and when we eat together, our brains receive the message that we are safe and happy. Our bodies are then flooded with positive hormones and emotions. Having a meal with your friends and family is a great way to boost your mood. So, next time your friend is feeling down, suggest the two of you go out for dinner. Benefits to eating with your friend and taking them out to dinner include:

- **Share Experiences Together and Bond:** Exploring a new restaurant together creates a unique shared experience that can serve as a lasting memory that acts as a stepping stone in growing a stronger bond between you and your friend.

- **Learn New Recipes:** You can learn new recipes and get excited about healthy ingredients when you dive headfirst into cuisine you have never tried before. Or it could even be cuisine you have tried but with a difference or two in how it was prepared. Going to new restaurants is a great way to expand your palate and find out what you like and what you don't! Consider finding a new cuisine and challenging one another to cook it on a night you stay in for the evening!

- **Develop a Sense of Adventure:** Exploring a new restaurant together can evoke a sense of adventure, excitement, and curiosity, leading to a fun and memorable experience for both of you.

- **Participate in Mutual Exploration:** This goes along with developing a sense of adventure, but it's a little more than that. Mutually exploring the unknown gives you both the opportunity to step outside of your comfort zone and try something new together. This develops a sense of teamwork.

- **Strengthen Your Trust in One Another**: Sometimes it isn't easy to step out of your comfort zone. And maybe your friend chooses a restaurant that is the complete opposite of what you would usually go for. Choosing a restaurant involves mutual decision-making and depends upon trusting and respecting one another's preferences—which is a great exercise in developing a solid relationship. Going in together and sharing a meal can help strengthen your trust in one another. You're both in it together, and worst-case scenario: the food is gross and you still did something fun with your friend. But you never know when you're going to have an amazing culinary experience. Allowing your friend to choose a restaurant and sharing the experience with them, regardless of whether you like the food or not, is a great exercise in mutual decision-making and fosters trust and understanding in each other's preferences.

- **Develop a Respect for Differences:** It allows for an appreciation of each other's tastes and preferences, which in turn promotes a level of respect by accepting differences from your friend.

- **Find a Little Novelty and Excitement in Something Completely Normal:** Experiencing a new restaurant introduces novelty and excitement into your routine, breaking up monotony and injecting just a smidgen of freshness into your friendship. Trying different cuisines or atmospheres broadens your horizons and encourages a sense of open-mindedness, which we could all use a little more of.

- **Enjoy One Another's Company and Relax:** Ultimately, sharing a meal in a new environment provides an opportunity to relax and enjoy good food with good company. What could be better?

Don't forget to shake things up a bit. Don't be afraid to try new ethnicities of food. Also don't be afraid to change from a food truck one day, to a Michelin-star dining experience the next. By experiencing a variety of culinary experiences, you and your friend can break the boundaries of your comfort zones, leading to an enriching bonding experience.

- **Equality:** Taking turns in planning activities or outings ensures that the responsibility is shared equally. It prevents one person from feeling burdened or the other feeling neglected in the friendship.

- **Diversity:** Each individual brings unique interests and ideas to the table. By rotating the planning, you get to explore a variety of activities and experiences that cater to both your preferences.

- **Strengthened Connection:** Participating in each other's planned activities promotes a deeper understanding and appreciation for each other's interests. It creates opportunities for shared memories and strengthening bonds.

Ways you can implement taking turns, especially if one person has generally taken the reigns previously include:

- **Cooking or Baking:** Experimenting with new recipes or baking homemade treats that you saw online or on TV can be fun and delicious.

- **Gardening:** Gardening is not only a relaxing hobby but can also lead to beautiful results.

- **Painting or Drawing:** Explore your artistic side by taking up painting, drawing, or other forms of visual art. You can create your own art or attend art classes. Now there are even "painting with a twist" classes that involve wine and other fun elements.

- **Hiking or Nature Walks:** Enjoy the great outdoors by going on hikes or nature walks in local parks or nature reserves. It's an excellent way to stay active and appreciate nature.

- **Photography**: Capture moments and memories by taking up photography. You can explore your surroundings and document your adventures together.

- **Playing Musical Instruments**: Learning a new instrument together can be difficult, but also incredibly rewarding! Consider taking joint classes and jamming together!

- **Birdwatching**: Birdwatching can be a relaxing and educational hobby. Get a pair of binoculars and observe the various bird species in your area. Put up a few feeders nearby and enjoy them up close, as well.

- **Knitting**: Learning how to make your own garments or blankets can be fun and can give you and your friend a chance to catch up and talk while you make them!

- **Wine or Beer Tasting**: If you're of legal drinking age and appreciate beer or wine, you can explore different wineries or breweries together.

- **Puzzle Solving:** Work on jigsaw puzzles, crosswords, or brain-teasers together. Puzzle-solving can be a mentally stimulating and enjoyable pastime. There are subscription boxes you can sign up for, too, and make it a monthly ritual to solve a new one together!

- **Dancing**: Learn different dance styles such as ballroom, salsa, or swing dancing. You can take classes or learn from YouTube.

- **Book Club:** Start a book club and read and discuss books together. This is an excellent way to share your thoughts and insights on various literature—and it can even open up the door to more in-depth and meaningful discussions.

- **Yoga or Meditation:** We discussed that self-care is important, and yoga and meditation is a great two-for-one. You can practice self-care and participate in great quality time with your friend if you do it together! Use it as a way to stay healthy and reduce stress and if you want to make it extra fun, attend a class together.

- **Volunteer Work**: Find a cause or organization each of you is passionate about and sign up to volunteer. This is a meaningful way to give back to the community together.

- **Stargazing**: Bring the chairs and the snacks and spend evenings stargazing and identifying constellations. Consider investing in a telescope for a more in-depth celestial exploration, and keep track of events happening in your viewing area.

- **Model Car Building**: Pick up an old craft such as building model cars! Any kind of craft that you are each interested in would work well as a hobby or activity that you and your friend can bond over.

- **Home Improvement:** Collaborate on home improvement projects or DIY renovations. This can be a productive and satisfying way to upgrade your living space. Branch out, too, and potentially earn extra cash in the meantime.

- **Travel**: Plan and take trips together. Make sure you're exploring new places, cultures, and cuisines since this is all about trying new things together and truly experiencing things with one another. Traveling can create unforgettable shared experiences.

Remember that the key to a successful shared hobby is to choose activities that all parties can enjoy and that align with everyone's interests and abilities. Be especially careful to really make sure that whatever you and your friend choose, you're able to experience it for the first time, together, and that you stay consistent and keep at it!

Be Reliable

Reliability is the cornerstone of strong relationships. It encompasses consistency, trustworthiness, and a commitment to being a present and supportive friend. To be reliable means to be:

- **A Consistent Presence:** Reliable individuals show up consistently, not just physically, but emotionally and mentally, for their friends and family. Think of those friends who are unwavering pillars of support—those who stand by you through thick and thin, celebrating your victories and offering solace during hardships. Be like them. Be a consistent presence with your friends, too.

- **Someone with Honesty and Integrity:** Honesty is pivotal in being reliable. In fact, you cannot be reliable if you're dishonest or operate without integrity. True friends speak the truth with compassion and integrity, offering constructive criticism and encouragement. They keep you grounded without resorting to belittlement or one-upmanship.

- **Committed to Follow-Through:** Reliable friends are true to their word. That's part of what makes them so trustworthy. They do what they say and say what they mean! They follow through on their commitments, ensuring that their actions align with their promises. Their reliability instills a sense of true dependability.

- **Someone who Contributes to the Well-Being of Others:** In a balanced friendship, both parties contribute to each other's well-being. Reliable friends reciprocate support, guidance, and encouragement to their friends. They do not solely take but actively give back. Make sure that you are giving back to your friend and contribute to their overall well-being.

- **Respectful:** Respecting a person and their values is crucial for reliability in friendships. Your values are your guiding principles, and friends who respect or share those values contribute to a strong and dependable relationship. Influencing someone to compromise their values makes you unreliable and untrustworthy.

Being a reliable friend is to be a trustworthy friend. Ways to express reliability include:

- **Setting Clear Expectations:** Communicate openly about what reliability means to you in your friendships. Clarify expectations regarding commitments, honesty, and support for one another.

- **Communicating Honestly:** Practice honest communication, providing constructive feedback when necessary. Be a source of encouragement and empowerment, uplifting your friends while being truthful.

- **Reciprocating Support:** Contribute to your friends' well-being by offering support and encouragement. And always be there when they need you the most. Build a balanced and mutually supportive relationship.

Be Flexible

Flexibility is a quality that empowers us as human beings to adapt, evolve, and navigate life's unpredictable circumstances with a better sense of ease. It's an essential skill that allows for a complete openness to change. An ability to pivot when necessary and the resilience to face challenges head-on is a skill that a lot of employers look for, but it's also pretty effective in your friendships, too, because you have no idea what sort of events can occur in your relationship.

Cultivate a Growth Mindset

A key component of flexibility is having a growth mindset. Embrace challenges as opportunities for growth and learning rather than viewing them as only obstacles. As frustrating as they may be, try to be open to new ideas, experiences, and perspectives.

Practice Adaptability

Learn to adapt to new situations and environments. Recognize that change is inevitable, including in friendships. Being adaptable allows you to adjust your mindset and actions accordingly. Embrace change as a chance for personal development. You never know, something amazing might be around the corner; and a change that might have been viewed as negative initially might end up being something wonderful in the long run.

By being flexible, you can develop skills such as:

- **Problem-Solving Skills:** By being flexible you can enhance your problem-solving skills to handle unexpected situations effectively in the future. Focus on finding solutions rather than dwelling on problems. Break down complex issues into manageable parts and explore various strategies to resolve them.

- **Being Open-Minded:** By maintaining an open mind and being willing to consider different viewpoints, you will be able to explore alternative approaches and solutions that you might not have initially considered.

- **Resilience:** People who are flexible have an incredible level of resilience which equips them well to maintain healthy relationships. Understand that setbacks are a natural part of life and use them as opportunities to learn and grow stronger. This helps you develop coping mechanisms to bounce back from challenges, which in turn strengthens your overall efficiency in relationships.

- **Learning How to Appropriately Prioritize:** Have you ever heard the phrase, "Your priorities aren't in check?" If you are a flexible person or practice flexibility, that's something that you likely won't have to hear. Assessing situations and tasks helps determine their importance and urgency. By being able to adapt your plans, you can properly deduce which areas of your life to prioritize. This aids in relationships because it helps you develop a sense of intuition similar to the one determining what to prioritize in a relationship.

Be Willing to Compromise

The most important aspect of being flexible is being able and willing to compromise with your friend during any situation. Be open to negotiation and finding a solution that can benefit both of you. This helps foster collaborative efforts in your relationship and allows both parties to truly get involved.

Remain Patient and Persistent

Being flexible in any given situation doesn't always yield immediate results. It is important to practice patience and persistence when faced with challenges or when implementing changes in a relationship. Stay committed to your—and your friend's—goals while being adaptable in your approach.

Celebrate Progress, Not Perfection

Acknowledge and celebrate victories and progress that is made between the two of you, no matter how small, even if things don't go exactly as planned. Embracing flexibility means understanding that perfection is not always attainable, but progress is incredibly valuable.

Revisit Places of Significance

Consider revisiting a place that is important to both you and your friend, as this is at times some of the best medicine you can give to your friendship. Revisiting places that hold special meaning for both of you can oftentimes rekindle fond memories. Going back to places where you've shared significant moments can evoke nostalgia and remind you of the journey you've taken together. It may even remind you why you love your friend in the first place.

These places are part of your shared life together and revisiting them reinforces the idea that you've built something meaningful over time—a true relationship. Reliving positive experiences can be beneficial to both your friend's and your mental health. Make the most out of revisiting by:

- Planning Together: Discuss which places hold the most meaning for each of you. It could be the place where you first met, a place where you had your first friend vacation or getaway, your childhood town, a baseball field you used to play in, or anything that holds significance to you.

- Schedule Visits: Make plans to visit these kinds of places periodically. You can schedule a day trip or weekend getaway to spend quality time there. Definitely consider making these sorts of revisits part of an anniversary tradition or ritual.

- Create New Memories: Don't always rely on your nostalgia to get you through. When you go back to these special places, make sure that you're trying to create new memories together there.

- Share Reflections: Talk about your feelings and memories associated with these places. This is a great bonding exercise.

- Stay Present: While revisiting, stay present in the moment. Put away your cell phone and focus on only each other.

Key Takeaways:

In chapter seven, we learned that all friendships need a bit of social element to survive. Friendships are often enriched through shared social experiences, steadfast support, and the willingness to embrace life's journey together.

We learned in this chapter that supporting your friend comes in various shapes in sizes such as:

- **Going to the Gym:** Engaging in shared physical activities such as exercising together not only promotes health but also fosters mutual encouragement and unity toward a common goal: becoming better, well-rounded human beings—together.

- **Letting Them Confide in You:** Providing a safe space where friends feel comfortable confiding and sharing with each other creates an environment of trust and deepens the emotional connection that the two of you have.

- **Being Their Cheerleader:** This means more than just cheering for them when they succeed. It also means pushing them to succeed. It means pushing them further than they believed they could go because you believe in them and what they have to offer.

In addition to supporting your friend, it's important to just sit back, and enjoy the ride from time to time when socializing with them. You can do that by:

- **Laughing Together:** Inside jokes can help you laugh and enjoy one another and knit together a shared experience that serves as an almost intimate interaction. Continuing to have these sorts of experiences with your friend keeps the relationship fresh and maintains a level of camaraderie in the deepest sense.

- **Discovering New Culinary Delights:** Exploring new restaurants or relishing meals together becomes an adventure, too, that can serve to spice up the bond the two of you have. Infusing shared memories with culinary delight can truly be a rewarding experience, because not only do the two of you get to enjoy something together and experience something for the first time as friends, but you also get something tasty out of it.

- **Revisiting Places of Significance:** Everyone has a favorite place to go or somewhere that harbors a fond memory. Remember to revisit these areas as they can hold a special bonding experience for both of you.

And finally, remember that to be a great friend, you must harbor dual traits to truly solidify the trust in your relationship. These are reliability and flexibility. Always make sure that your friends can depend on you, and make sure to bend to fit their needs as much as possible.

Chapter Eight

Chapter 8: Final Thoughts

As we conclude this journey exploring the myriad ways to cultivate and nurture a loving relationship with your friend, it's crucial to reflect on the profound significance of these connections in our lives. What does your friend bring to the table? Do their emotional strengths complement yours and do yours them? The very fact that you have picked up this book means that you have some sort of motivation or desire to strengthen your relationship with them. Perhaps you can start by learning to lean on them for support and companionship. The complexities of friendship dynamics and their ever-shifting presences often require patience, understanding, and an unwavering commitment to not only establish but to maintain genuine bonds with one another.

Above Everything Else, Communicate

Throughout this book, we've delved into the depths of understanding personality types, highlighting the contrasting traits of the Cave Dweller (CD) and the Mountain Yeller (MY). Recognizing these differences isn't merely a means of classification but a pathway toward empathy. It allows us the opportunity to comprehend and appreciate the varying perspectives that every unique person brings to the table.

If you take nothing else from this guidebook, take the importance of communication. Communication emerges as the cornerstone of any thriving and healthy relationship. We've emphasized the importance of expressing feelings without igniting conflicts, the art of active listening, and the power of employing neutral language to foster an environment free from defensiveness.

Setting clear expectations and being open about your shifting friendship dynamics lays the groundwork for building trust and understanding within your relationship. So set clear expectations and boundaries, and above all else, show your friend that you love and appreciate them the best way you can—using this guide to help you demonstrate that love as effectively as possible.

After all, with love comes attachment. In fact, attachment is known to be a component of love. Strong attachment bonds set us apart from other animals and allow us to socialize through life with others. it doesn't matter how long you've known your friend, how you met, or how often you see each other. What matters is the attachment you have with them now, and the one you can grow through mutual respect, understanding, communication, and yes, love.

We Are All Human

As we discussed in this guide, a funny thing happens when you become an adult. You finally start to realize that other people are human, too. There will always be an opportunity for conflict as long as there is an opportunity for growth. Make sure that you continue to give your friend the benefit of the doubt, love them despite their flaws, and understand that they are likely doing their best at any given moment.

They make mistakes, just as you do, and you have to understand that you must set your expectations to a realistic standard. You also need to put your relationship with your friend to a realistic standard. Nurturing your bond every single day is important, but it isn't very realistic the older we get. As life's obligations pile up, loving your friend can quickly fall to the bottom of the to-do list. This is okay!

Make sure that you're keeping in touch as often as you can and still communicating and expressing your love for one another. It doesn't have to entail grandeur or extravagance. Sometimes it can be a small text message that says, "thinking of you".

Prioritizing time together—truly quality time—will ensure that your friend feels heard, understood, accepted, and loved. Mix that with small acts or gestures of surprise and kindness and you can truly build a strong foundation that won't be harmed by a missed day or thirty of communication.

Respect Differences

Ultimately, navigating relationships—especially ones that take the backseat at times—takes time, practice, and lots of communication and effort. Remember that you and your friend are separate people. Your friend likely has different priorities, values, or goals than you do. That's also perfectly okay! They don't have to always agree with you, and you don't have to always agree with them. But take responsibility for the fact that it is also up to you to navigate these situations with dignity and respect.

In fact, if you treat these differences with the respect that they deserve, it is likely that your friend will be much more receptive to seeing things from your perspective in the future. You can be honest about who you are and what's important to you without being dismissive of their beliefs.

Take Responsibility

If you want to set boundaries in your adult relationships, make sure that you're respecting their boundaries and respecting their opinions and differences. When you make a mistake, own it, and apologize for it sincerely without pointing fingers. Remember, you don't have to apologize for everything that happened but always apologize for your part in it.

Stop Making Assumptions

Conflicts can quickly erupt in relationships because people make assumptions about what someone wants or how they will react to any given situation. For example, you shouldn't assume your friend doesn't have plans and will drop everything to do something with you when you decide. Likewise, even if something is a "usual" thing for you and your friend, don't assume that they can make it every time. For example, if the two of you have gotten into a routine of going out for brunch every Sunday, don't assume that it is a tradition that can't be broken just because it's something the two of you have been doing regularly. Have that conversation and remember that relationships are two-way streets.

Both of you have to agree to something before it's written in stone. You should respect their time, just as you would expect them to respect yours. Instead, share your desire to spend time together and communicate what you'd like to accomplish. This will make your relationship with your friend a lot easier to navigate in the future and give you both the opportunity to grow and develop the relationship accordingly.

Stay in Contact and Practice Being Present, Even When There's Conflict

Being around each other every day is likely not going to happen with you and your friend as you get older and move in different directions. That means time together should be cherished. Make sure that you're completely present when you do spend time with one another. It is also worth mentioning that there is a difference, and you need to know what that difference is. Being truly present in another person's life means involving yourself in their hopes, dreams, accomplishments, and everything in between. It also means showing genuine care and empathy when they face challenges. And this is all for better or worse.

Loving someone is a choice that you have to make every day. When things are tense with a friend it can be all too easy to not return a phone call or to just leave them on "read" in your text thread. You may be thinking that as an adult, you're free to cut off contact whenever you feel like it, with whoever you feel like. However, it is important to note that unless a relationship is abusive or toxic to your mental health you should never cut off contact. Avoiding them may feel like the appropriate choice in the moment, and it may honestly feel therapeutic, but it's not wise. Not only are you cheating yourself out of an opportunity to grow and mature as a human by facing the conflict, but you're also harming your relationship by damaging the trust. Trust is everything in a relationship, no matter what kind. So, continue to choose to love your friend, even through disagreements. You can take a moment to breathe and take a step back to assess your emotions and feelings when arguments or disagreements arise, but always promise to come back to the discussion at another time. Your relationship depends on consistency and effort. So, choose to love your friend, and make that conscious choice every day to show them that you're worthy of their trust, their respect, and their overall affection.

Chapter Nine

Appendices

Self-Assessment Questionnaire: Determine if You're a CD, MY, or Straddler.

In the quest for self-understanding, recognizing one's intrinsic personality traits plays a crucial role. This self-assessment questionnaire has been carefully designed to help you discern whether you align most closely with the introspective nature of a Cave Dweller (CD), the extroverted inclinations of a Mountain Yeller (MY), or the balanced characteristics of a Straddler. By reflecting on your behaviors, preferences, and reactions in various situations, this tool aims to provide insight into your predominant personality type. Approach each question with honesty and openness, and remember, there's no right or wrong answer – just a deeper understanding of your unique self waiting to be unveiled.

Personality Indicator #1

Circle one answer per question.

1. Have you ever walked in your sleep during your adult life?

YES or NO

2. As a teenager, did you feel comfortable expressing your feelings to one or both of your parents?

YES or NO

3. Do you have a tendency to look directly into a person's eyes when talking to them?

YES or NO

4. Do you feel that most people, when you first meet them, are uncritical of your appearance?

YES or NO

5. In a group situation with people you've just met, would you feel comfortable drawing attention to yourself by initiating a conversation?

YES or NO

6. Do you feel comfortable holding hands or hugging someone you're in a relationship with in front of other people?

YES or NO

7. When someone talks about feeling warm physically, do you begin to feel warm also?

YES or NO

8. Do you tend to tune out when someone is talking to you because

you're anxious to come up with your side of the story?

YES or NO

9. Do you feel that you learn better by seeing and/or reading than by hearing?

YES or NO

10. In a new class or company meeting, do you usually feel comfortable asking questions in front of the group?

YES or NO

11. When expressing your ideas, do you find it important to relate all the details leading up to the subject so the other person can understand it completely?

YES or NO

12. Do you enjoy relating to children?

YES or NO

13. Are you comfortable with your body movements when faced with unfamiliar people and circumstances?

YES or NO

14. Do you prefer reading fiction rather than non-fiction?

YES or NO

15. If you were to imagine sucking on a juicy lemon, would your

mouth water?

YES or NO

16. Do you feel comfortable receiving a compliment in front of other people?

YES or NO

17. Do you feel that you're a good conversationalist?

YES or NO

18. Do you feel comfortable when complimentary attention is drawn to your physical body?

YES or NO

Personality Indicator #2

Circle one answer per question.

1. Have you ever awakened in the middle of the night and felt that you could not move your body and/or talk?

YES or NO

2. As a child, did you feel you were more affected by your parents' tone of voice than by what they actually said?

YES or NO

3. If someone you know talks about a fear that you've experienced before, do you have a tendency to re-experience that

apprehension or fear?

YES or NO

4. After having an argument with someone, do you tend to dwell on what you could or should have said?

YES or NO

5. Do you tend to occasionally tune out when someone is talking to you and therefore don't hear what's being said because your mind drifts to something totally unrelated?

YES or NO

6. Do you sometimes desire to be complimented for a job well done but feel embarrassed or uncomfortable when complemented?

YES or NO

7. Do you often fear not being able to carry on a conversation with someone you've just met?

YES or NO

8. Do you feel self-conscious when attention is drawn to your physical body or appearance?

YES or NO

9. If you had a choice, would you rather avoid being around children most of the time?

YES or NO

10. Do you feel uptight in body movements, especially when faced with unfamiliar people or circumstances?

    YES or NO

11. Do you prefer reading non-fiction rather than fiction?

    YES or NO

12. If someone describes a very bitter taste, do you have difficulty experiencing the physical feeling of that bitter taste?

    YES or NO

13. Do you generally feel that you see yourself less favorably than others see you?

    YES or NO

14. Do you tend to feel awkward or self-conscious holding hands and/or kissing someone you're in a relationship with, in front of other people?

    YES or NO

15. In a new lecture or company meeting, do you usually feel uncomfortable asking questions in front of the group?

    YES or NO

16. Do you feel uneasy if someone you've just met looks you directly in the eyes when talking to you, especially if the conversation is about you?

YES or NO

17. In a group situation with people you've just met, would you feel uncomfortable drawing attention to yourself by initiating a conversation?

    YES or NO

18. If you're in a relationship or are very close to someone, do you find it difficult or embarrassing to verbalize your love for them?

    YES or NO

Personality Indicator Scores

Personality Indicator #1

- Give yourself 10 points for every "yes" answer for questions 1 and 2.
- Give yourself 5 points for every answer for questions 3–18.
- Write the total number at the top of #1's questionnaire.

Personality Indicator #2

- Give yourself 10 points for every "yes" answer for questions 1 and 2.
- Give yourself 5 points for every answer for questions 3–18.
- Write the total number at the top of #2's questionnaire.

- Combine the total from PIs 1 and 2.

Using the Scoring Chart

On the scoring chart, look up the combined score of Personality Indicators 1 and 2 on the HORIZONTAL axis of the chart and circle the number.

- Take the total score of PI #1, locate it on the VERTICAL axis of the chart, and circle the number.

- Draw a horizontal line across the page from the PI 1 score, then draw a vertical line down from the combined score.

- The number in the box where the two lines intersect represents your true, adjusted percentage personality indicator.

- Scores 61 and higher indicate a Mountain Yeller personality type.

- Scores 45 and lower indicate a Cave Dweller personality type.

- Scores 47–56 indicate a Straddler personality type.

Cave Dweller Tendencies

- Reserved

- Head ruled

- Controlling

- Wants space and security

- Prefers socializing one-on-one

- Singular focus

- Thinks before reacting
- Prefers showing affection privately
- Distrusts flattery
- Enjoys working alone
- Enjoys individual activities
- Wants alone time
- Dresses for comfort
- Decides after thinking about it
- Speaks literally—to the point
- Infers from what others say
- Feels emotional pain in the mind
- Fears loss of security

Cave Dweller Priorities

- Career/Financial Security
- Hobbies/Children
- Relationships/Family
- Sex/Lovers

Mountain Yeller Tendencies

- Outgoing
- Heart ruled
- Dominating
- Wants connection and touch
- Enjoys socializing in groups
- Moving focus
- Reacts spontaneously
- Comfortable with affection anytime
- Likes reassurance and compliments
- Enjoys working with people
- Enjoys team activities
- Wants to be together as much as possible
- Decides in the moment
- Speaks inferentially—adds story
- Takes literally what others say
- Feels emotional pain in body and mind
- Fears rejection

Mountain Yeller Priorities

- Relationships/Sex
- Family/Children
- Friends/Hobbies
- Career/Financial security

SCORE # 1

0	5	10	15	20	25	30	35	40	45	50	55	60	65	70	75	80	85	90	95	100	
0	10	20	30	40	50	60	70	80	90	100											50
0	9	18	27	36	45	55	64	73	82	91	100										55
0	8	17	25	33	42	50	58	67	75	83	92	100									60
0	8	15	23	31	38	46	54	62	69	77	85	92	100								65
0	7	14	21	29	36	43	50	57	64	71	79	86	93	100							70
0	7	13	20	27	33	40	47	53	60	67	73	80	87	93	100						75
0	6	13	19	25	31	38	44	50	56	63	69	75	81	88	94	100					80
0	6	12	18	24	29	35	41	47	53	59	65	71	76	82	88	94	100				85
0	6	11	17	22	28	33	39	44	50	56	61	67	72	78	83	89	94	100			90
0	5	11	16	21	26	32	37	42	47	53	58	63	68	74	79	84	89	95	100		95
0	5	10	15	20	25	30	35	40	45	50	55	60	65	70	75	80	85	90	95	100	100
0	5	10	14	19	24	29	33	38	43	48	52	57	62	67	71	76	81	86	90	95	105
0	5	9	14	18	23	27	32	36	41	45	50	55	59	64	68	73	77	82	86	91	110
0	4	9	13	17	22	26	30	35	39	43	48	52	57	61	65	70	74	78	83	87	115
0	4	8	13	17	21	25	29	33	38	42	46	50	54	58	63	67	71	75	79	83	120
0	4	8	12	16	20	24	28	32	36	40	44	48	52	56	60	64	68	72	76	80	125
0	4	8	12	15	19	23	27	31	35	38	42	46	50	54	58	62	65	69	73	77	130
0	4	7	11	15	19	22	26	30	33	37	41	44	48	52	56	59	63	67	70	74	135
0	4	7	11	14	18	21	25	29	32	36	39	43	46	50	54	57	61	64	68	71	140
0	3	7	10	14	17	21	24	28	31	34	38	41	45	48	52	55	59	62	66	69	145
0	3	7	10	13	17	20	23	27	30	33	37	40	43	47	50	53	57	60	63	67	150
0	3	6	10	13	16	19	23	26	29	32	35	39	42	45	48	52	55	58	61	65	155
0	3	6	9	13	16	19	22	25	28	31	34	38	41	44	47	50	53	56	59	63	160
0	3	6	9	12	15	18	21	24	27	30	33	36	39	42	45	48	52	55	58	61	165
0	3	6	9	12	15	18	21	24	26	29	32	35	38	41	44	47	50	53	56	59	170
0	3	6	9	11	14	17	20	23	26	29	31	34	37	40	43	46	49	51	54	57	175
0	3	6	8	11	14	17	19	22	25	28	31	33	36	39	42	44	47	50	53	56	180
0	3	5	8	11	14	16	19	22	24	27	30	32	35	38	41	43	46	49	51	54	185
0	3	5	8	11	13	16	18	21	24	26	29	32	34	37	39	42	45	47	50	53	190
0	3	5	8	10	13	15	18	21	23	26	28	31	33	36	38	41	44	46	49	51	195
0	3	5	8	10	13	15	18	20	23	25	28	30	33	35	38	40	43	45	48	50	200

COMBINED SCORE #1 AND #2

About the Author

Dr. Cline lives with her husband, two daughters, two German Shepherds, and two Yorkies in the hills of North Carolina. Her expertise in relationship building has offered her the opportunity to travel around the world as a keynote speaker and international workshop facilitator.